Come, Lord Jesus!

HE NATIVITY OF OUR
LORD OR THE BIRTH-
DAY OF Christ COM-
MONLY CALLED
CHRISTMAS-DAY

Geoffrey Rowell is the Bishop of Gibraltar in Europe. Formerly Chaplain of Keble College, he is the author of numerous scholarly and devotional books including *Flesh, Bone, Wood* published by the Canterbury Press. He was one of the compilers of *Love's Redeeming Work: The Anglican Quest for Holiness* published by Oxford University Press.

Julien Chilcott-Monk is a musician and writer living in Hampshire. He was the co-author of *Flesh, Bone, Wood*.

Come, Lord Jesus!

Daily readings for
Advent, Christmas, and Epiphany

Geoffrey Rowell and
Julien Chilcott-Monk

MOREHOUSE PUBLISHING
A Continuum imprint
HARRISBURG • LONDON • NEW YORK

First North American Edition 2003

Morehouse Publishing
4775 Linglestown Road
Harrisburg, Pennsylvania 17112
www.morehousepublishing.com

Morehouse Publishing is a Continuum imprint.

Scriptural quotations are from the Catholic Edition copyright © 1965 and
1966 of the Revised Standard Version of the Bible copyright © 1946, 1952,
and 1957 by the Division of Christian Education of the National Council of
Churches in the USA. Used by permission. All rights reserved.

Illustrations gratefully received from the private collection of Julian W. S. Litten.

Library of Congress Cataloging-in-Publication Data

Come, Lord Jesus! : daily readings for Advent, Christmas, and Epiphany /
[compiled by] Geoffrey Rowell and Julien Chilcott-Monk.
    p. cm.
  ISBN 0-8192-1964-9 (pbk.)
  1. Advent—Prayer-books and devotions—English. 2. Christmas—
Prayer-books and devotions—English. 3. Epiphany—Prayer-books and
devotions—English. I. Rowell, Geoffrey. II. Chilcott-Monk, J. P.
  BV40.C54 2003
  242'.33--dc21

                                                    2003002706

        03 04 05 06 07 08   6   5   4   3   2   1

Contents

Preface

In our previous book, *Flesh, Bone, Wood* (Canterbury Press, 2000) the passion, death and resurrection of Jesus was explored by endeavouring to enter imaginatively into the reactions and feelings of many of those involved in the story. It built on a tradition of Christian meditation which has a long history. Passages for reflection were drawn for the most part from sermons, addresses and meditations on passion themes that I have given throughout my ministry both as chaplain for many years at Keble College, Oxford, and as a bishop. Julien Chilcott-Monk was largely responsible for the selection of the passages and for the daily ordering and meditation of the particular one of the *dramatis personae* on which the day focussed. In this Advent and Christmas book a similar pattern is followed, with the reflection material coming from my Advent and Christmas sermons, addresses and meditations, and the selection of the passage, the daily ordering and meditation (in this instance frequently in the person of Mary), together with the quotations from traditional liturgical material, the introits, antiphons and sequences being the responsibility of Julien Chilcott-Monk. We hope and pray that *Come, Lord Jesus!* will enable those who use it to enter more fully into the mystery of the incarnation in which God joined together things earthly and heavenly in the Child of Bethlehem, who was laid on pricking straw in the manger, foreshadowing the nails and piercing of Calvary. Mary his Mother also journeyed from Bethlehem to Calvary, fulfilling Simeon's prediction that a sword would pierce her own soul also. In this book we find ourselves with her in order that like her we may find ourselves in an ever-closer union with her Son.

† Geoffrey Rowell

How to Use This Book

Come, Lord Jesus! is a preparation for and celebration of the Nativity and the Epiphany of Our
Lord, and provides material for daily meditation
and prayer from November 27 (Day 1) – the earliest date for Advent Sunday – to January 6 (Day
41), the Feast of the Epiphany. One further day's
material (Day 42) is provided for Candlemas on
February 2. It is our hope that this book will
encourage profound exploration and contemplation, but it is not, perhaps, a conventional
Advent book of readings and prayers, for that the
reader will have to look elsewhere.

    Come, Lord Jesus! is a series of spiritual exer-
cises to give light and foundation to each day's
thoughts and, in the cumulative effect of forty or
so days, to deepen one's capacity to begin to
understand something of the Incarnation. As such,
the book is, of course, related to the imaginative,
meditative tradition of Ignatian spirituality. Daily,
the reader is invited to stand beside Mary, the
mother of Jesus, as she sits in the outer precinct of
the temple recalling and pondering the events of
the first dozen years of her son's life. She sits here
having found Jesus disputing with the doctors,
lawyers and wise men of the temple, waiting to
begin once again the return journey to Nazareth.
Her ponderings are made from that perspective:

we, however, hear her thought sin the light of our knowledge of the ministry, crucifixion and resurrection of Jesus.

But before we listen to Mary we have in front of us: a passage of Scripture; comment for the purposes of elucidation; reflection, in order to open the door to other avenues of thought; and an appropriate portion from, usually, the *Proper of the Sarum Mass*, common currency until the Reformation. Mary's musings are sometimes observations on the Scripture; sometimes a development of previous thoughts. Finally, a point or question for application, self-examination or consideration, is then provided either to stand alone or to serve as a mnemonic with which to associate the various strands of the day's contemplation. For as long as time permits, the mind ought to be given free rein to enter completely into the drama of it all and of the extraordinary and wonderful will of the heavenly Father.

It is entirely a matter for the reader, but it is suggested that the daily session begin in prayer – for example, the Gloria Patri and the Paternoster – and end in prayer – for example, an Ave Maria and the Collect for the day. However, something less formal and less rigid may be preferred. To assist the meditation, it may be helpful to have set before one a painting or icon of the annunciation or of the nativity, and a crucifix.

Julien Chilcott-Monk

Introduction

This series of meditations running from the beginning of Advent up to Christmas, and then on to Epiphany and Candlemas, belongs to what the Orthodox theologian, Thomas Hopko, has called 'The Winter Pascha'.[1] Lent books enabling us to enter more deeply into the mystery of Love's redeeming work in the passion, death and resurrection of Jesus are well known; Advent books are less so. Yet there is no reason why this should be. The birth narratives of the Gospels of Matthew and Luke are, even in today's secularised society, among the passages of Scripture most widely known. Carol services and nativity plays keep alive the memory of that moment of incarnation that T.S.Eliot called 'the intersection of the timeless with time'.[2]

The moment of incarnation is, of course, not Christmas but the annunciation. The great paintings, so vividly portrayed by St Luke, of Gabriel's angelic greeting to Mary, have something of the quality of Michaelangelo's creation of Adam in the Sistine Chapel. There the space between the creative hand of God and the reaching out hand of Adam speaks imaginatively of God creating out of nothing, bringing into being the creature other than himself yet made in his image and likeness. So, in the Annunciation paintings the space between angel and virgin, and the gestures of Gabriel reaching out and Mary's awesome acceptance of her vocation, sometimes inclining in reverence to the angel, sometimes almost shrinking away, point to that moment when, as Lancelot Andrewes said, God went 'to the very groundsill of our nature'.

Words on wings, the Word announcing
Uttered from the depths of love,
Word which from the world's beginning
Longed to dwell at one with us,
So the Father's Word creative
Fashioned is in human form,
In our world becomes a native
Is for our salvation born.

At those awesome words of greeting,
'Hail, O Virgin, full of grace!'
Mary shrinks in awed obedience
Gives herself as dwelling-place,
To the God who gave her being
Framed the boundless realms of space
Who in outpoured love's self-giving
Takes our human heart and face.

Mary becomes the Mother of the Saviour by God's shaping and preparing providence, and by the overshadowing of the Holy Spirit (Luke 1.35). As the cloud, the *Shekinah*, of the divine glory covered the tabernacle in the wilderness, 'and the glory of the Lord filled the tabernacle' (Exodus 40.32) so Mary is the tabernacle which is to be filled with the glory of God. 'The *Almah* (the young woman of Isaiah's prophecy) has conceived, the glory of the Lord, the *Shekinah*, has entered – and no more a wooden but a living tabernacle; the prophecies have begun to be fulfilled ... Lowliness and glory, obedience and exaltation, these are the paradoxes of the divine election, which made of the humble Virgin of Nazareth the Mother of the Son of the Most High.'[3]

In the devotion of the Eastern Churches Mary is hailed as the one who is 'greater than the Cherubim and incomparably more glorious than the Seraphim'.[4] She is defined by the Council of Ephesus (431), a council which the Church of England has traditionally accepted, as the *Theotokos*, the God-bearer, for that must be so if the child she bore is none other than God incarnate. Her bearing of the promised Messiah is the beginning of God's new creation, when God enters into his creation, 'taking the form of a servant, born in the likeness of man' (Philippians 2.7). This *kenosis*, or self-emptying of God is God identified with us, entering into human genealogy and lineage (cf. The genealogies of Jesus in Matthew and Luke, and the stress on Jesus as the Son of David) but no less in the fact of the virgin birth marking a new beginning. For many of the Fathers of the Church it is this that marks the importance of Mary's miraculous conceiving and child-bearing rather than the physical ministry as such, even though piety could seek to protect and exalt Mary's unique role with the assertion that in childbirth she retained her virginity and was 'ever-Virgin.'[5]

In Coptic devotion, Mary is iconographically portrayed as the virgin giving her breast to her Son. This is sometimes assimilated to ancient Egyptian portrayals of Isis giving suck to her son Horus. The virgin is hailed as the new tabernacle, Jacob's ladder joining earth and heaven, the burning bush on fire and not consumed, the golden censer, and the dove of Israel (the Coptic *shoupsou* onomatopoeically suggests the cooing of the dove). Any Old Testament figure or incident indicative of the presence, grace, indwelling and saving power of God is regarded as legitimate symbolism to apply to Mary, within whose womb and through whose co-operation, the incarnate Lord was born.

In the mid-second century the *Protevangelium of James* elaborated the story of Mary, recalling how she was born to aged parents, Joachim and Anna, a child of promise. At six months her mother set her down and unaided she walked seven steps (a sacred number). At the age of three she was presented in the Temple and was placed on the third step of the altar. 'And the Lord cause grace to descend upon her, and she danced with her feet, and all the house of Israel loved her.'[6] Mary is linked with the Temple and with the weaving of purple thread for the Temple, and some annunciation iconography depicts Mary engaged in this task when she is startled by Gabriel's appearance.

The scenes of Mary's childhood first elaborated in the *Protevangelium of James* were depicted by artists in the Christian East, a notable example being in the last flowering of Byzantine art in the church of St Saviour in Chora (the Holy Saviour in the Fields) built by Theodore Metochites in the fifteenth century just inside the great Byzantine walls of Constantinople, from which the city had at that time shrunk, leaving the new church in the fields.

Marian devotion in the West was powerfully shaped by the increasing stress on the humanity of Christ in the twelfth century. St Bernard in his Christmas sermons meditates on the physical discomfort of the birth of Christ. Later, St Francis of Assissi is credited with the origin of the Christmas crib, first created at Greccio in 1223 to set the scene of the Lord's birth before the faithful to kindle their devotion. Since that time cribs have become familiar features of Christmas, whether in the elaborately carved wooden cribs of Bavaria, or the *mechanico praesepio* of many churches in Rome, replete with moving stars, journeying Magi, flights of chorussing angels and elaborate landscape settings for the holy family and the manger. Victorian England saw a revival of the cult of the holy family and melded with the German custom of the decorated Christmas tree to provide many elements of what is thought of as the traditional Christmas.[7] Handel's *Messiah* (1741) and Bach's *Christmas Oratorio* (1734) provided musical meditations on the mystery of the incarnation linking Old Testament texts to New in prophecy and fulfilment. In a different way the nine lessons and carols, first introduced at Truro Cathedral by

E. W. Benson in 1880 and re-shaped by Eric Milner White at King's College, Cambridge in 1918, plot an imaginative response to the nativity story, and carols continue to be both discovered and composed. John Tavener's compositions have brought new influences from the Orthodox east into the Christmas repertoire.

It is against this rich background, in which the Church, like Mary, 'keeps all these things and ponders (*sumballo* – literally symbolises) them in her heart', that this series of meditations seeks to deepen our devotion and understanding, and to draw us into a deeper Christian commitment in faith and life as we journey through Advent to Candlemas. It is right that we should do so by sharing imaginatively in the vocation of Mary as God unites himself so closely with her human life, and she learns what it is to be the God-bearer, for her vocation is ours also. William Law once wrote that 'a Christ not in us is a Christ not ours.' Bishop Phillips Brooks taught us to sing and pray that the child of Bethlehem would be born in us.

> *O Holy Child of Bethlehem*
> *Descend to us we pray,*
> *Cast out our sin and enter in*
> *Be born in us today.*
> *We hear the Christmas angels*
> *Their great glad tidings tell:*
> *O come to us, abide with us,*
> *Our Lord Emmanuel.*

'Even so, come, Lord Jesus!'

[1]Thomas Hopko, *The Winter Pascha: Readings for the Christmas-Epiphany Season*, New York: St Vladimir's Seminary Press, 1984

[2]T.S.Eliot, *Four Quartets*, 'Little Gidding' London: Faber, Library ed., 1985, p. 36

[3]Hilda Graef, *Mary, A History of Doctrine and Devotion*, Christian Classics, London: Westminster/Sheed & Ward, Combined ed., 1985, I, pp. 10, 12

[4]Liturgy of St John Chrysostom

[5]Graef, op. cit. pp.

[6]*Protevangelium* 7.2, q. Graef, op.cit., p.36

[7]Cf. Geoffrey Rowell, 'Dickens and the Construction of Christmas,' *History Today*, 43, December 1993, pp.17–24.

Come, Lord Jesus!

Day 1

(27 November – the earliest date for Advent Sunday)

The Revelation to John (The Apocalypse) 22 : 12, 13, 16, 17, 20, 21

'Behold, I am coming soon, bringing my recompense, to repay everyone for what he has done. I am the Alpha and the Omega, the first and the last, the beginning and the end.'

'I Jesus have sent my angel to you with this testimony for the churches. I am the root and the offspring of David, the bright morning star.'

The Spirit and the Bride say, 'Come.' And let him who hears say, 'Come.' And let him who is thirsty come, let him who desires take the water of life without price.

He who testifies to these things says, 'Surely I am coming soon.' Amen. Come, Lord Jesus!

The grace of the Lord Jesus be with all the saints. Amen.

(Almighty God is revealed in Christ Jesus; Jesus sends an angel to the writer; and the writer himself bears witness in his book.)

Reflection

Throughout the weeks of Advent we shall consider again the Creation, the Fall of man, the call of Abraham and of Moses; and let us hear the voice of the prophets. And all this will point us towards Christmas, that coinciding of God with us in a single life, in a human birth: God in swaddling cloths on a mattress of straw. But into this consideration breaks an older theme, linked deep down with the sense of the dying of the year, the darkness pressing in, the last leaves fluttering wrinkled and brown from the bare branches. Our forefathers thought of this time of the winter solstice as the time when the sun itself might die, and so life come to an end. Therefore, the midwinter festivals are those which seek to re-kindle hope, because the dying of the year brings to mind our own inevitable dying. As we face the horizon of the year's end, we face the horizon of our own ending, and of the world's ending.

The famous *Dies Irae* sequence – *Day of wrath, O day of mourning* – belonged first to the Advent season before it became part of the Requiem and Liturgy of Burial. However, the old themes of Advent – Death, Judgement, Hell and Heaven, the Four Last Things – echo this sense of the dying year, but now sit uneasily with our customary anticipation of Christmas.

The mid-winter festival of *Sol Invictus*, the unconquered sun, kept on 25 December, just after the shortest day, was an affirmation of hope in the life and light which was to return. In taking that day as the celebration of the coming into the world of Christ the true sun, radiant with the light and glory of God's love and grace, the Church baptized and hallowed the festival.

Just as the light of Easter breaks into the darkness of Lent, so the light of Christmas breaks into the darkness of Advent. The ending, the horizon, which bounds our lives and bounds the world, is God the Alpha and Omega of all things. He it is whom we encounter at our death; he is the one by whom we are judged: to be separated from him is hell; to live in the light and joy of his presence is heaven.

The Sequence: *Dies Irae*

Day of wrath, O day of mourning, lo! the world in ashes burning; seer and Sibyl gave the warning.
O, what fear man's bosom rendeth, when from heaven the Judge descendeth, on whose sentence all dependeth.
Wondrous sound the trumpet flingeth, through earth's sepulchres it ringeth, all before the throne it bringeth.

Mary:

I recall, during the early stages of my pregnancy, that I was anxious to begin my vocation; to give birth to my son – to begin! But I soon came to realize that I had already begun my work, as my commission was truly alive within me. God's incredible plan had come into effect from the moment of God's 'overshadowing'. Nevertheless, from time to time I found myself whispering earnestly: 'Come, Lord Jesus!'.

For further consideration . . .

I exist within the completeness of God, who is the beginning and the end.

Day 2

The Gospel of Mark 13:5–8a, 12, 13

And Jesus began to say to them, 'Take heed that no one leads you astray. Many will come in my name, saying, "I am he!" and they will lead many astray. And when you hear of wars and rumours of wars, do not be alarmed; this must take place, but the end is not yet. For nation will rise against nation, and kingdom against kingdom; there will be earthquakes in various places, there will be famines . . . And brother will deliver up brother to death, and the father his child, and children will rise against parents and have them put to death; and you will be hated for my name's sake. But he who endures to the end will be saved.'

The Gospel of John 11 : 17, 21a, 24b–27

Now when Jesus came, he found that Lazarus had already been in the tomb four days. Martha said to Jesus, 'I know that he will rise again in the resurrection at the last day.' Jesus said to her, 'I am the resurrection and the life; he who believes in me, though he die, yet shall he live, and whoever lives and believes in me shall never die. Do you believe this?' She said to him, 'Yes, Lord; I believe that you are the Christ, the Son of God, he who is coming into the world.'

(Jesus calls for steadfastness throughout political upheaval and natural phenomena. 'I am' is a pregnant phrase – in the Old Testament, for example, it represented the glory and person of Almighty God himself.)

Reflection

There is, of course, a difference in attitudes to death and the experience of death between earlier ages and our own. Until late in the nineteenth century, every man and woman would have had at least one experience of death close at hand before the age of ten; that is, death as the cutting short of life, not as a merciful release. Death, today, is, for the most part, not at home but behind screens in hospital and shut away. It is as frightening as in the Middle Ages with the grim picture of the Dance of Death, but frightening because unknown.

Death proportions us. This horizon of death runs across the lives of all of us and none of us can avoid it. Perhaps we are sometimes beguiled into thinking we have a more absolute and complete control over our lives than we do, by not thinking of the dying that comes to us all.

In the book of Genesis, in the great story of Adam's Fall, the expulsion of Adam and Eve from the Garden of Eden – of Paradise – leads not only to toil and to hardship, but also to death. Death is understood as a consequence of separation from God, who is the source of life. But at the heart of that great song of victory and triumph that is the Easter gospel is the theme of the death of death and the destruction of hell. The resurrection of Jesus is the breaking of new life out of the grave, the turning of death into the gateway to immortal life. The Christian perspective on life is now a perspective with a new and ultimate horizon. Beyond the horizon of our dying is the horizon of resurrection life, the new and eternal life which is the gift of God in Jesus Christ. Our horizons have changed, so that for us it is God himself, in his love, his glory and his goodness, who is our horizon, the goal towards which we are travelling and the end of all our exploring. He holds us all in life and brings us by his grace to those unspeakable joys which are the very life of heaven.

The Sequence: *Dies Irae*

Death is struck, and nature quaking, all creation is awaking, to its judge an answer making.
Lo! the book exactly worded, wherein all has been recorded; thence shall judgement be awarded.
When the Judge his seat attaineth, and each hidden deed arraigneth, nothing unavenged remaineth.

Mary:

What would the presence of the 'Son of the Most High' mean to mankind? I wondered day and night. And I still wonder as I watch him grow: perhaps I can see something of the future in his mature grasp of argument here in the Temple. But will evil still appear to reign, and men continue to

fight against brother and against neighbour? Or
will it be that God's word will have immediate
effect through my son?

For further consideration . . .

Lazarus was brought back to life: he would die
again. Christ rose from the dead to die no more;
death would have no more dominion over him.

Day 3

The Gospel of Matthew 24 : 29–31, 36, 44

'Immediately after the tribulation of those days the sun will be darkened, and the moon will not give its light, and the stars will fall from heaven, and the powers of the heavens will be shaken; then will appear the sign of the Son of man in heaven, and then all the tribes of the earth will mourn, and they will see the Son of man coming on the clouds of heaven with power and great glory; and he will send out his angels with a loud trumpet call, and they will gather his elect from the four winds, from one end of heaven to the other. But of that day and hour no one knows, not even the angels of heaven, nor the Son, but the Father only. Therefore you also must be ready; for the Son of man is coming at an hour you do not expect.'

(See also the Parable of the Ten Maidens, Matthew 25:1–13)

Reflection

What do we discern at the final horizon of the world's history? Many early Christians, and many Christians throughout Christian history, would have spoken simply of the second coming of Christ; his return in glory to judge the living and the dead. One should not think that it is a live possibility for us to speak simply of the second coming of Christ.

The pictorial framework of Jewish apocalyptic writing is just that, and highly colourful and imaginative it is. If, as seems likely, the earliest Christians thought that this language conveyed a literal account of things to come, then they were destined to disappointment. And, almost certainly, one of the shaping elements in the construction of the New Testament as we have it is their coming to terms with this not happening as soon as they had expected.

As Christians we live in Christ, and so share with him his vision of the future as that which belongs to God; we share likewise his resource of the life of God, his self-giving love, which in transforming us enables the future to be transformed into the kingdom of Christ. 'At the end he shall examine thee in love' said St John of the Cross; and in the first letter of John we read: 'Here and now, dear friends, we are God's children; what we shall be has not yet been disclosed, but we know that when it is disclosed we shall be like him, because we shall see him as he is.' That is the Christian future, and that is our Advent hope.

The Sequence: *Dies Irae*

What shall I, frail man, be pleading, who for me be interceding, when the just are mercy needing? King, of majesty tremendous, who dost free salvation send us, fount of pity then befriend us.

Think, kind Jesu, my salvation caused thy wondrous incarnation; leave me not to reprobation.

Mary:

My duty is clear, and in that I am most fortunate, though I cannot help but speculate about other matters. I suspect that had Almighty God desired a sudden, crashlike, thunderous, spectacular change he would have done so in a shaft of lightning, an earthquake or some other grand phenomenon and not in the still small voice, not in the birth of a child. He has worked in many extraordinary ways throughout the history of mankind; and yet, is the birth of a child extraordinary in any way?

For further consideration . . .

No one would have believed that five of the maidens, having spent so long preparing for the wedding feast, could have been so stupid – and that is the point.

Day 4

'When the Son of man comes in his glory, and all the angels with him, then he will sit on his glorious throne. Before him will be gathered all the nations, and he will separate them one from another as a shepherd separates the sheep from the goats, and he will place the sheep at his right hand, but the goats at the left. Then the King will say to those at the right hand, "Come, O blessed of my Father, inherit the kingdom prepared for you from the foundation of the world; for I was hungry and you gave me food, I was thirsty and you gave me drink, I was a stranger and you welcomed me, I was naked and you clothed me, I was sick and you visited me, I was in prison and you came to me." Then the righteous will answer him, "Lord, when did we see thee hungry and feed thee, or thirsty and give thee drink? And when did we see thee a stranger and welcome thee, or naked and clothe thee? And when did we see thee sick or in prison and visit thee?" And the King will answer them, "Truly, I say to you, as you did it to one of the least of my brethren, you did it to me." Then he will say to those at his left hand, "Depart from me, you cursed, into the eternal fire prepared for the devil and his angels; for I was hungry and

*you gave me no food, I was thirsty and you gave
me no drink, I was a stranger and you did not welcome me, naked and you did not clothe me, sick
and in prison and you did not visit me." Then they
also will answer, "Lord, when did we see thee
hungry or thirsty or a stranger or naked or sick or
in prison, and did not minister to thee?" Then he
will answer them, "Truly, I say to you, as you did
it not to one of the least of these, you did it not to
me." And they will go away into eternal punish-
ment, but the righteous into eternal life.'*

(See also the Parable of the Talents – Matthew
25 : 14–30. The use of the word 'talent' for skill,
strength or gift arises from this parable.)

Reflection

The qualities of beauty, what is personal, what is
free and what is sheer gift are all part of what we
mean by the grace of God. The contrast is often
made in the Bible between 'law' and 'grace' –
between the strict obligations of moral demand
(which is good) and that which goes beyond that
moral demand – God's accepting love, his forgiveness and mercy, his overwhelming free gift, his
loving-kindness. Such grace transforms situations,
delivers from sin, heals our brokenness, floods our
hearts with light and encircles us in the communion of love.

But no matter how compelling and how powerful the lure of God's love may be, we are free to
choose not God, and may choose ourselves. Hell,

therefore, is the ultimate aloneness, because it is the self-centred willing and choosing which in the end excludes all other and refuses communion. If heaven is the communion of love, hell is its absence. Because love is meaning, hell is lack of meaning, darkness, chaos, and an isolation which may indeed be annihilation.

Those who choose hell have their reward: those who choose heaven find, as Paul puts it, 'all things are theirs', 'for you are Christ's and Christ is God's.' To speak of heaven is to speak of God as our goal and our end, and our ultimate meaning.

The Sequence: *Dies Irae*

Righteous Judge of admonition, grant thy gift of absolution 'fore that reckoning day's conclusion.
Worthless are my prayers and sighing, yet, good Lord, in grace complying, rescue me from fires undying.
With thy favoured sheep, O place me; nor among the goats secure me, but to thy side please upraise me.

Mary:

Or are the days of my son to be characterized by judgement; by the sifting of the good and the bad; the punishing of the sinner; the rewarding of the just? Surely God can do that in the calm and in the storm without employing the agency of my son? Is it my place to say so? No, of course not.

Is Jesus to establish the New Eden so that

mankind can realize God's original intention for his creation? If so, mankind will have to turn, to respond.

For further consideration . . .

The King is concerned with the reality of response to human need, not our tally of engagements.

Day 5

The Book of the Prophet Isaiah 11:1–4a, 6, 9

There shall come forth a shoot from the stump of Jesse, and a branch shall grow out of his roots. And the Spirit of the Lord shall rest upon him, the spirit of wisdom and understanding, the spirit of counsel and might, the spirit of knowledge and the fear of the Lord. And his delight shall be in the fear of the Lord.

He shall not judge by what his eyes see, or decide by what his ears hear; but with righteousness he shall judge the poor, and decide with equity for the meek of the earth . . .

The wolf shall dwell with the lamb, and the leopard shall lie down with the kid, and the calf and the lion and the fatling together, and a little child shall lead them. They shall not hurt or destroy in all my holy mountain; for the earth shall be full of the knowledge of the Lord as the waters cover the sea.

(If the whole earth is filled with those who know God, the cessation of brutality will be a natural consequence.)

Reflection

Heaven, even when thought of as the dwelling-place of God, is also the divine order which perfectly expresses the creative purpose of God. To be a creature is to be made for heaven. When the psalmist sees all the created order giving glory and praise to God, he recognizes both the creatureliness of all that is, and that its true purpose is only discerned when it is seen as sustained in existence by God's creative power. The Eastern Christian tradition, in particular, stresses this same point when it speaks of the saints as those who are privileged to see the creation as transfigured by the Divine Light. We, too, are created; we share this same dependence upon and orientation towards the divine order; but our human nature is made 'in the image of God' with the capacity for freedom, creativity and love, which reflects that of God himself. So of us it is the case, in Augustine's famous words, that 'God has made us for himself, and our hearts are restless until we rest in him.' For us, that divine order which is heaven, is seen to be the perfect communion with God, who in calling us into being for himself, also gave himself to be in our condition, in the identification of love which is that perfect communion.

The Sequence: *Dies Irae*

Low I kneel with heart-submission; see, like ashes, my contrition, help me in my last condition.
Guilty, now I pour my sadness, all my shame with

sorrow, hapless: spare, O God, thy suppliant's badness.

Thou the sinful Mary* savest, thou the dying thief forgavest, and to me a hope vouchsafest.

Mary:

I cannot always grasp the cumulative effect of the prophets' utterances because they sometimes appear to compete with one another, if not – dare I say it – contradict one another.

What will Jesus bring to the world? Will he embody all the prophets' words? How can he? We are taught that the prophets are speaking to us as much as to our forefathers. Will my son herald a general reckoning as he assembles mankind and parades it before his Father? As a saviour, is he then mankind's example, advocate and *redeemer*?

For further consideration . . .

The little child – the Christmas Child – is now to be seen as the shepherd leading a flock of unlikely souls.

* *Mary Magdalene*

Day 6

The Book of the Prophet Jeremiah 23:1–6

'Woe to the shepherds who destroy and scatter the sheep of my pasture!' says the Lord. Therefore thus says the Lord, the God of Israel . . . You have scattered my flock, and have driven them away, and you have not attended to them. Behold, I will attend to you for your evil doings . . . Then I will gather the remnant of my flock . . . I will set shepherds over them who will care for them, and they shall fear no more, nor be dismayed, neither shall any be missing . . . Behold, the days are coming . . . when I will raise up for David a righteous Branch, and he shall reign as king and deal wisely, and shall execute justice and righteousness in the land. And in his days Judah will be saved, and Israel will dwell securely. And this is the name by which he will be called: "The Lord is our righteousness."'

(In a later insertion, the writer adds that those days will be thought of as greater even than God's deliverance of the Children of Israel from Egypt.)

Reflection

The judgement of others; the judgement of ourselves; we find ourselves continually concerned with these. But in writing to the Christians of Corinth Paul points them to the judgement of God. 'My judge is the Lord. So pass no premature judgement; wait until the Lord comes. For he will bring to light what darkness hides, and disclose men's inward motives.' Paul probably expected the return of the Lord in judgement to take place almost immediately, so part of his message is that the time is too short to be concerned with our pettiness and, in any case, all human judgement will soon be set aside. Therefore, Paul says, wait for the true and final judgement to take place. Such an immediate return of the Lord did not happen, so we cannot ourselves simply take up this position. But Paul's main point remains. It is the judgement of God which is important, and which is the only judgement that matters, for only God really understands, only God really knows, and only God really loves us as we are. For this reason the judgement of God is something we should desire, for it is the only judgement adequate to our humanity; and that judgement is also the judgement of love. We shall fall short; we know we are unloving; that our love has limits and boundaries; that we do not love with the love of our Lord. Yet that same love by which we are judged and found wanting is that which reaches down to us in our need, to draw us to the heart of God, and to enflame our lives. Christ our Lord is Saviour and judge. That same love is measured by the cross of Christ, where it is anchored in the harsh reality of the world's evil and man's suffering. By his cross the righteousness and justice of God are seen to be but the burning fire of his love. To be judged by God is to know that in everything we are in need of his acceptance and forgiveness, and the healing of his love. To understand this is to enter into the Christian life by the door of humility, and know that our worth consists solely in the fact that we are loved by God – than which nothing can be more marvellous.

The Sequence: *Regnantem sempiterna*

Let the choir devoutly bring welcome to the eternal King, and with one consent renew the Creator's homage due.

Awesome he in judgements deep, yet in might doth mercy keep; by thine agony of woe pity, Lord, and save us now.

Bid the universe be pure, let us live in peace demure, till unto those realms we rise where thou reignest ever wise.

Mary:

There is little doubt in my mind, as I sit here in the outer precinct of the Holy Temple, that God, through his prophets, has inveighed against those who have been given the responsibility for leading his people but who have led them astray. Are we all culpable, however? Is the responsibility shared?

Does my son, at this moment, show something of what is to come? Did the prophets look to this day? And is it possible only to understand their admonitions and prophesies in the light of the present?

For further consideration . . .

I must take care when my responsibility is, even momentarily, that of a shepherd.

Day 7

The Book of the Prophet Zechariah 9:9, 11, 12, 14a, 16, 17a

Rejoice greatly, O daughter of Zion! Shout aloud, O daughter of Jerusalem! Lo, your king comes to you; triumphant and victorious is he, humble and riding on an ass, on a colt the foal of an ass. As for you also, because of the blood of the covenant with you, I will set your captives free from the waterless pit. Return to your stronghold, O prisoners of hope; today I declare that I will restore you double. Then the Lord will appear over them . . . On that day the Lord their God will save them for they are the flock of his people; for like the jewels of a crown they shall shine on his land. Yea, how good and how fair it shall be!

(The 'waterless pit' means the barren wastes of exile and, by extension, a mind that is not open to God's will.)

Reflection

Advent is a time of expectancy. Most popularly it is a time of expectancy looking forward to the feast of the incarnation, of God's coming among us as one of us. But Advent is also the time of expectancy in its sharp reminder of the Christian longing for the fulfilment of all things. The end of the world has indeed a note of judgement about it, because for a sinful and fallen world to encounter God inevitably means judgement. But the end of the world is also the bringing to an end of all that is evil, and a time of final victory and triumph, of new creation. The Revelation to John portrays dramatically in strange visionary language the final conflict between good and evil, the costliness of God's victory, and the defeat and annihilation of the powers of evil. It also rejoices in both the triumphant worship of the heavenly places where the great company of the redeemed sing praise to God, and looks forward to the new creation in the vision of the heavenly city, the new Jerusalem, the city that comes down from God out of heaven like a bride adorned for her bridegroom. That great hope of new life, of new community, of new hope, is summed up simply in the prayer that is very nearly the last word of the Bible – 'Even so, come, Lord Jesus!' That longing for the coming of Jesus, who is the new creation, the one in whom we are made new, is echoed in that little Aramaic prayer, which must have meant so much because it was preserved in the Greek-speaking churches for many decades: 'Maranatha!' – 'Come, Lord!'.

The Introit: *Rorate caeli*

Drop down ye heavens from above, and let the skies pour down righteousness; let the earth open, and bring forth a Saviour.

Mary:

We always love to hear, to look forward to what God has in store for us one day: do we comprehend – do *I* comprehend – that this day actually will dawn, indeed has already dawned? A benevolent father's promise of a special gift is engendered. How would he choose *me* to be the vehicle for that great gift? In all humility, it sometimes seems absurd, and yet God has always surprised and worked in ways not necessarily comprehensible to human beings. I rejoice!

For further consideration . . .

I am called to be one of those jewels, reflecting from my face the Christness within.

One Good Shepherd

Day 8

The Book of the Prophet Zechariah 10 : 3a, 6b, 8, 12

'My anger is hot against the shepherds, and I will punish the leaders; for the Lord of hosts cares for his flock . . . I will bring them back because I have compassion on them, and they shall be as though I had not rejected them; for I am the Lord their God and I will answer them. I will signal for them and gather them in, for I have redeemed them, and they shall be as many as of old. I will make them strong in the Lord and they shall glory in his name,' says the Lord.

(Both the Jewish leaders and the foreign powers responsible for the Jews in exile are referred to as 'shepherds'. If 'shepherds' fail in their duty of care, they will be judged accordingly.)

Reflection

Often, the image of Jesus the Good Shepherd is one of cosy sentimentality and we miss the true significance of the title – particularly living as we do in a society so very different from that out of which that title sprang. In the Middle East today, shepherds and their flocks are still very much an integral part of society and the point of our Lord's title can in that setting be forcibly brought home. The shepherd rises at dawn, sometimes having slept uncomfortably out in the cold night air; he leads or drives his flock to the nearest water-hole, and then to some scrubby pasture; in the blistering heat of the day he keeps perpetual watch for predators; he rounds up and searches for the thirsty and lost stragglers in the evening. It is emphatically not a job for the weak, but one for the strong.

Once we imaginatively project ourselves into such a society, we can grasp just how apt and vivid the image of the shepherd was to the men of the ancient Middle East. The image of the shepherd is that of a strong ruler, who cares for his people, and is concerned for their protection and safety even at risk to himself. It is no surprise, therefore, that in the Old Testament God's care for his people is expressed many times in terms of a shepherd's care for his flock. 'The Lord is my shepherd, therefore shall I lack nothing' is the most familiar example of all. God cares for his people with the same care that the shepherd has for his flock, with the same costly devotion. But because it is God who cares for us and watches over us even in our darkness and pain and dull incomprehension of his presence, we can meet whatever comes with a sure trust in his loving-kindness – that searching and sensitive concern for his people in which the prophets and psalmists so often rejoice.

The Gradual: *Qui sedes*

Thou, O Lord, that sittest upon the cherubim, stir up thy strength and come. Hear, O thou shepherd of Israel, thou that leadest Joseph like a sheep. Stir up, O Lord, thy strength and come and help us.

Mary:

Why, I wonder, does God continue to love his people? Certainly, he has earmarked them and set them aside whilst giving choice to the whole of mankind. Since our descent from Adam and Eve, man continues to choose badly, to make the wrong choice, not through ignorance of the correct path but through the ignoring of the Divine will.

If the shepherds lead God's people along the paths of the wicked for their own corrupt ends, is judgement not likely to be swift and sure?

Is my son to be the one Good Shepherd?

For further consideration . . .

If 'they shall be as many' then my vocation is clear.

Day 9

The Book of the Prophet Haggai 2 : 4b–7

'Take courage, all you people of the land, says the Lord; work, for I am with you, says the Lord of hosts, according to the promise that I made you when I came out of Egypt. My Spirit abides among you, fear not. For thus says the Lord of hosts: Once again, in a little while, I will shake the heavens and the earth and the sea and the dry land; and I will shake all nations, so that the treasures of all nations shall come in, and I will fill this house with splendour, says the Lord of hosts.'

(We can take the last sentence as God's call to all nations to come to him.)

Reflection

When the prophets, seized by this active love and care of God, looked for ways of speaking of the hope of his future coming to save his people, it was to this picture of the shepherd they often turned. So Jesus is the Good Shepherd because in him God's loving-kindness, his self-giving care for his people, is perfectly expressed. His action and that of his Father are one, and so he is not only shepherd but also the door of the sheepfold, the way, the truth, and the life, by which men may come to their true home. His care and his love are individual, as the shepherd's is for the flock; his voice is the one we recognize, because the word spoken to us is the creative word which calls us to life.

The Sequence: *Qui regis sceptra*

Thou who dost each earthly throne rule by thy right hand alone, raise up thy great power and shine, shew thy flock thy face divine.
Saving gifts on him bestow whom the prophets did foreshow, from the palace ever high, Jesu, to our land draw nigh.

Mary:

Throughout our history God has dealt patiently and mercifully with us, punishing us, as a father punishes his children, by removing us from the lands promised from of old. Others have occupied these lands as they do now. Will humanity ever be able to perfect itself by bending its own will to God's?

For further consideration . . .

With the spreading of the knowledge of the Lord, the souls of the people of all nations become 'the treasures of all nations.'

Day 10

The Book of the Prophet Isaiah 35:4–6a, 8, 9, 10b

Say to those who are of a fearful heart, 'Be strong, fear not! Behold, your God will come with vengeance, with the recompense of God. He will come and save you.' Then the eyes of the blind shall be opened, and the ears of the deaf unstopped; then shall the lame man leap like a hart, and the tongue of the dumb sing for joy. And a highway shall be there, and it shall be called the Holy Way; the unclean shall not pass over it, and fools shall not err therein. No lion shall be there, nor shall any ravenous beast come up on it; they shall not be found there, but the redeemed shall walk there. They shall obtain joy and gladness, and sorrow and sighing shall flee away.

(This is quoted by Jesus in answer to the question brought from prison by John the Baptist's disciples.)

Reflection

In the prophets' utterances, God is angry with the shepherds for failing in their duty, and they look forward to a shepherd capable of the task. He is identifiable with the Messiah and in the days ahead he will be heralded by a forerunner, and his days will be characterized by the turning upside down of the normal pattern of life. In answering the question about his identity from the imprisoned John, Jesus draws attention to the seeing eyes and the hearing ears.

But Jesus, the Good Shepherd, goes beyond the Old Testament hope, beyond its picture of God as the shepherd of his people, for he lays down his life for the sheep – his love and his care break through the constraints of the shepherd's care, to reach down to our utmost need. And this giving of his life is done in the full freedom of the love out of which it arises; and the glory of that love is the cross and the resurrection.

The Sequence: *Eia recolamus*

The very Godhead is in human flesh arrayed: what ear of earthly witnesses hath heard such things essayed?
To seek that which was lost the Shepherd good came down.

Mary:

I remember as I rejoiced with Elizabeth, we remarked upon God's infinite ability to perform the unexpected; to turn the world upside down; to do with his creation contrary to what is expected of his creation or contrary to what is known of the nature of his creation.

For further consideration . . .

Only the redeemed walk there because humanity is redeemed: all who walk are redeemed.

Day 11

The Book of the Prophet Malachi 3:1–3a

Behold, I send my messenger to prepare the way before me, and the Lord whom you seek will suddenly come to his temple; The messenger of the covenant in whom you delight, behold, he is coming, says the Lord of hosts. But who can endure the day of his coming, and who can stand when he appears?

For he is like a refiner's fire and like fullers' soap; he will sit as a refiner and purifier of silver . . .

(We see this clearly as a perfect description of the Baptist, and the passage was cited by Mark at the beginning of his Gospel.)

Reflection

'What did you go out into the wilderness to see?' Jesus asks his hearers. Was it something in nature, a reed swaying in the wind perhaps? No. Was it a man of rank, with all the trappings of fine clothes and high living? Again, no. What attracted the crowds to the wilderness was none of these things, it was the enigmatic figure of John the Baptist. Here was a man whose insight into the issues of life penetrated to the heart of the matter. Here was a man who was utterly convinced of the activity of God in the world, not in some remote period, but here and now, at the present moment. Here was a man who, because of this, was able to challenge men and women in the duplicity of their motives and the shallowness of their lives, calling them to a new beginning. It was for this that they went into the desert. And it is John who points the way to Jesus with 'Behold, the Lamb of God.' For the Good Shepherd is also the Lamb who is slain; our great High Priest is also the Victim.

The Introit: *Gaudete*

Rejoice in the Lord always: and again I say, Rejoice. Let your moderation be known unto all men. The Lord is at hand. Be careful for nothing; but in all things by prayer and supplication let your requests be made known unto God.

Mary:

The correction and purification of humanity is a constant theme; the building and rebuilding of the Temple; the breaking down, the raising up. My early years were dedicated to this Temple and I remember that the work of Herod the Great's grand plans took many years. Joseph was employed in this enlargement and reconstruction.

For further consideration . . .

Fullers' soap was an agent in the shrinking, washing and bleaching of new cloth. It was the effect rather than the procedure that interested the Prophet Malachi.

Day 12

(8 December – The Immaculate Conception of Mary)

The Book of the Birth of Mary 1:1–3a; 2:1b, 3a, 6, 9, 10

The blessed and ever glorious Virgin Mary, sprang from a royal race and the family of David, was born in the city of Nazareth, and educated at Jerusalem, in the temple of the Lord. Her father's name was Joachim, and her mother's Anne. The family of her father was of Galilee and the city of Nazareth. The family of her mother was of Bethlehem. Their lives were plain and right in the sight of the Lord, pious and faultless before men.

The angel of the Lord stood by Joachim in a prodigious light. 'Do not be afraid, Joachim, nor troubled at the sight of me, for I am an angel of the Lord sent by him to you, that I might inform you that your prayers are heard. For the mother of your nation, Sarah, was she not barren? And yet, even in her old age, she brought forth Isaac, in whom a promise was made of a blessing to all nations. But if reason will not convice you that there are frequent conceptions in advanced years ... therefore Anne your wife shall bring you a daughter, and you shall name her Mary. She shall ... be devoted to the Lord from her infancy, and be filled with the Holy Spirit from her mother's womb.'

(One version of the text of the Book of the Birth of Mary was found in the collection of writings in the possession of Jerome, one of the ancient Fathers of the Church.)

Reflection

A conception is about a beginning, for it is where we all begin, as a tiny dot of the stuff of life carried in our mother's womb. That too is where our Lord began, and it is also where Mary his mother began. The life of the Mother of the Lord, the one through whom God chose to share our human nature, began in the darkness of the womb of Anne, her mother.

In our often harsh and unthinking age, unborn life is at a discount and abortion is a right to be decided for the benefit of the mother. In some circumstances, to be pregnant seems to be equated with having an illness or disease. But new life is to be cared for, to be honoured, and to have rights. The God who chose to be fashioned in the womb of Mary, and Mary who was prepared by that same God from the very beginning for her vocation of motherhood, remind us why we should care for the unborn and fight for the life hidden in the womb. God prepared Mary, giving her the same grace from the beginning as he gives us in our baptism, and nothing less.

The Sequence: *Inviolata*

Thou art pure, thou art chaste, thou art without stain, O Mary. Thou art the bright gate of heaven.

Mary:

Am I favoured for the task of bringing up the 'Son of the Most High' – my son – because my parents dedicated my early life for service here? (Indeed, it overawes me to consider that I myself was God's Temple for nine months!) Or was I always a part of God's plan? Had I been set aside from my very beginning?

For further consideration . . .

The later legends and stories about the Holy Family are simply eye-catching signposts pointing the way to the truth.

Day 13

The Book of Genesis 3 : 11b–13, 16, 17, 20, 24

The Lord God said: 'Have you eaten of the tree of which I commanded you not to eat?' The man said, 'The woman whom thou gavest to be with me, she gave me of the fruit of the tree and I ate.' Then the Lord God said to the woman, 'What is this that you have done?' The woman said, 'The serpent beguiled me and I ate.' To the woman he said, '. . . in pain you shall bring forth children . . .' And to Adam he said, 'cursed is the ground because of you . . .'

The man called his wife's name Eve, because she was the mother of all living.

He drove out the man; and at the east of the garden of Eden he placed the cherubim, and a flaming sword . . .

(This ancient tradition tells the hearer that people's lust for their own selfish will is the barrier they build between themselves and the love of God.)

Reflection

'Original' sin is both the first sin – Adam, Eve and the apple – and the sin which is the fundamental flaw in our human nature, the first or the primary root of all the particular manifestations of sin. St Paul sees sin as an inherent power or attraction which distorts our moral perspective and saps the strength of our will. 'The good I would I do not; the evil I would not that I do.' The psalmist says: 'Behold, I was shapen in wickedness' to underline the fact that all of us are born into a fallen, sinful condition. This is the sin of self-concern and self-centredness, the very antithesis of the Christian duty of love of God and neighbour, which is at the heart of the way of Jesus.

God redeems by the freely-given gift of grace all that is fallen and sinful, but first we must turn to him and repent, that is, turn away from sin.

The Sequence: *Salus eterna*

Thou for ever our salvation, thou the life of all creation, thou our hope of restoration, thou the never-failing light; grieving for man's loss impending, by the tempter's wiles pretending, camest down thine aid extending, leaving not the starry height.

Mary:

Adam and Eve disobeyed God. Humanity had everything they needed and more; and all this was lavished upon them. But it wasn't enough; they broke through the boundaries set for them – which were wide and generous – simply because they were there. Since then our history has been

cycles of dutiful obedience and indiscipline, pun-
ishment and redemption.

O where does my son fit in? Is he somehow a
New Adam?

For further consideration . . .

The cross is the self-esteem of Adam – I –
expunged.

Day 14

The Book of Genesis 22 : 1, 2, 9, 10, 11, 12, 18

After these things God tested Abraham, and said to him, 'Abraham!' And he said, 'Here am I.' He said, 'Take your son, your only son Isaac, whom you love, and go to the land of Moriah, and offer him there as a burnt offering upon one of the mountains of which I shall tell you.'

When they came to the place of which God had told him, Abraham built an altar there, and laid the wood in order, and bound Isaac his son, and laid him upon the altar, upon the wood. Then Abraham put forth his hand, and took the knife to slay his son. But the angel of the Lord called to him from heaven and said, 'Abraham, Abraham!' And he said, 'Here am I.' He said, 'Do not lay your hand on the lad or do anything to him; for now I know that you fear God, seeing you have not withheld your son, your only son, from me.'

'And by your descendants shall all the nations of the earth bless themselves, because you have obeyed my voice.'

(Not only is Abraham selflessly obedient, but he also listens to God for fresh insights.)

Reflection

The story of God's people, the Children of Israel, is a story of God's calling a people to be his own. Sometimes the Children of Israel respond in obedience, and sometimes – perhaps more often than not – they are wayward and rebellious, and deny the God who called them. And in the history of Israel, the prophets call them back time and time again, to their first love, to the God who called them to be his very own.

The prophets know that vocation is something that has to control their lives, and in some cases experience it as a burden. Jeremiah, for example, often protests about what God has called him to be. And yet God says to him: 'Before I formed you in the womb I knew you; I called you to be a prophet to the nations.' In the end, after the great history has been played out, from the testing of Abraham to the Roman Empire, God's dealing with his people focuses on a young woman, Mary of Nazareth, so that it has sometimes been suggested that we can think of the history of Israel as being rather like an hour-glass narrowing to Mary, the Mother of the Lord, and the Christ who is her son, and then widening into the life of the new people of God, who live in the power of the Spirit of Christ.

The Sequence: *Salus eterna*

In our flesh thy glory veiling, all on earth, in ruin failing, thou didst save by might prevailing, bringing joy to all our race.

Mary:

Abraham was called to be the father of the specially chosen people. God revealed himself to Abraham. Why did he choose a people from among the whole of his creation? Why did he need a special people? Are all peoples chosen?

This special people – the Children of Israel – descended from Abraham, Isaac and Jacob: he perhaps chose a plan, an intention, not a pre-existing family of people. It was yet another stage in his creation, and he would, thereafter, gradually reveal more of himself, little by little, to succeeding generations. He taught Abraham (and at this very moment, my son now disputes with the elders about these matters) that human life is a sacred and precious gift, when he caused the ram to be caught in the thicket.

For further consideration . . .

Morality is our respect for God's handiwork.

Throne of David

Day 15

The Book of the Prophet Isaiah 9 : 2, 6, 7

The people that walked in darkness have seen a great light; those who dwelt in a land of deep darkness, on them has light shined. For unto us a child is born, to us a son is given; and the government will be upon his shoulder, and his name will be called 'Wonderful Counsellor, Mighty God, Everlasting Father, Prince of Peace.' Of the increase of his government and of peace there will be no end, upon the throne of David, and over his kingdom, to establish it, and to uphold it with justice and with righteousness from this time forth and for evermore. The zeal of the Lord of hosts will perform this.

(Here the language of Isaiah is the language of affirmation – and it is affirmation of a certainty in that which is hoped for.)

Reflection

The familiar words of the Prophet Isaiah – 'For to us a child is born, to us a son is given' – offer hope as we look forward once again to the Christmas Feast. We should not lose sight of the fact that we shall be celebrating nothing other than the mystery of the incarnation, of God taking our nature, stooping to where we are, to redeem us and to save us and to catch us into the mystery of his love. In some Orthodox icons, Mary is often portrayed with her new-born son, not in a stable but in a cave, and sometimes that cave can seem like the mouth of hell. Christ descended into the womb of Mary, into the darkness of this world, and would indeed go even further – to death on a cross, and to Hades, the place of the departed. This reminds us that this birth is God's stooping down to save us, to raise us up into the love and life of God.

As Isaiah goes on to say: 'His name will be called Wonderful Counsellor, Mighty God, Everlasting Father, Prince of Peace.'

The Sequence: *Salus eterna*

Grant, O Christ, thine expiation, unto us thine own creation, take us for an habitation cleansed for thyself to grace.

Mary:

Although God's messenger stated clearly what my task would be, I experience a jumble of emotions when I hear the words of the Prophet Isaiah declaring the birth of a son to sit upon the throne of David; that this son would, however, be no ordinary king. I cannot help but shudder with apprehension, in awe, with excitement, in humility. Was Isaiah's message a message for the generations to come, indeed to this very generation?

Our people were then warring among themselves; they had divided in animosity, north against south; they piled waywardness upon waywardness; time and again they became estranged from God; time and again they strayed from the paths onto which the prophets had guided them.

Would my son be the great illuminator? Simeon certainly said so.

For further consideration . . .

'Peace' has many layers of meaning beneath the mere cessation of war.

Day 16

The Book of the Prophet Micah 5 : 2, 4

But you, O Bethlehem Ephrathah, who are little to be among the clans of Judah, from you shall come forth for me one who is to be ruler in Israel, whose origin is from of old, from ancient days. And he shall stand and feed his flock in the strength of the Lord, in the majesty of the name of the Lord his God. And they shall dwell secure, for now he shall be great to the ends of the earth.

(This passage is the one cited by the scholars in Herod's palace.)

Reflection

By one of those seemingly curious coincidences of circumstances and duty, Joseph and Mary are in Bethlehem for the birth of Jesus. A modest little town, Bethlehem was 'David's city' for there he had been born, and there anointed. Although it had been of greater significance during the intervening centuries, it was now, again, a modest little town in which God chose to empty himself into our humanity. God comes to us not in a display of power but as a new-born baby; he chooses not only Bethlehem but chooses to be born in an outhouse, in a pen for animals, maybe; and so he identifies himself in love with the outcast, and the homeless; he comes as one vulnerable and weak, and so stoops to be with us. When those who built the Church of the Nativity at Bethlehem fashioned its doorway, they made it so low that all who enter have to stoop to do so as a permanent reminder of God's action.

The Sequence: *Salus eterna*

By thy first humiliation grant us, Lord, justification; when again in exultation thou shalt come, O set us free.

Mary:

But how shall Jesus sit upon the throne of David? Isaiah's words paint a picture of something much more than even a benevolent kingship. Jesus was certainly born in David's own city and so out of Bethlehem he has come. The Prophet Micah also persuades me with his promised shepherd and I begin consistently to believe that Jesus will become the Good Shepherd. And to think, moments ago I admonished him for doing what he ought to be doing!

Truly, the prophets spoke for their own times and for the future, and slowly but surely, God revealed more of himself to his people through those prophets and through the very history of his people.

For further consideration . . .

Do I stoop grandly, as the hypocrites fasted?

Day 17

The Book of the Prophet Isaiah 60:1–6

Arise, shine; for your light has come, and the glory of the Lord has risen upon you. For behold, darkness shall cover the earth, and thick darkness the peoples; but the Lord will arise upon you, and his glory will be seen upon you. And the nations shall come to your light, and kings to the brightness of your rising. Lift up your eyes round about, and see; they all gather together, they come to you; your sons shall come from far, and your daughters shall be carried in the arms. Then you shall see and be radiant, your heart shall thrill and rejoice; because the abundance of the sea shall be turned to you, the wealth of the nations shall come to you. A multitude of camels shall cover you, the young camels of Midian and Ephah; all those from Sheba shall come. They shall bring gold and frankincense, and shall proclaim the praise of the Lord.

(The light (i.e. the Lord himself) is here and, therefore, it will attract the whole world; and foreigners will pay tribute and worship the Lord. See also Haggai, Day 9.)

Reflection

As Micah looks back to the significance given to Bethlehem by David's illustrious kingship, and how again that little town will be of use to God, so the writer, late in the Book of the Prophet Isaiah, sees the Hope of Israel as a brilliant light that will reach the darkest corners of the earth and its peoples. And this light of God's love that shines in our darkness shines first of all in the darkness of the Virgin's womb, as though pin-pointed by a laser beam of his radiant brilliance.

This surpassing wonder is of a God who does not stand aside, but comes down to us; and is of a meaning which goes far beyond the calculations of science, or the ideology of politicians. Only this God has the power to change and transform the world. Let us consider the part we have been called to play in the world as we prepare for our journey to Bethlehem.

The Sequence: *Salus eterna*

When in glory manifested thou the secret heart hast tested, in unsullied robes invested may we closely follow thee.

Mary:

Mercy, loving-kindness, faithfulness, justness, holiness and redeeming love have all been revealed as God's qualities. Are they embodied in my son? Is my son – the 'Son of the Most High' – imbued with all these characteristics? Can he be the culmination of all these revelations? Is this too much? Is this my fantasy, my fancy, or is it an extraordinary truth?

Later, in the book of Isaiah, the promised one would be a light to shine in the darkness of the world, (and, again, I think of Simeon's words) a light to which all peoples of the world would gravitate. So, in selecting a special people, God did so for the benefit of mankind generally, to help them all recover Eden. We were given glimpses of Eden in the promised land, but Eden was more – it was God's perfect intention. 'All *nations* shall do him homage' – and I well remember the sight of those camels and rich plenipotentiaries arriving at the Bethlehem house.

For further consideration . . .

By my words and actions, how easy is it to obliterate that light?

Day 18

The Gospel of Luke 1 : 12–17

And Zechariah was troubled when he saw the angel and fear fell upon him. But the angel said to him, 'Do not be afraid, Zechariah, for your prayer is heard, and your wife Elizabeth will bear you a son, and you shall call his name John. And you will have joy and gladness, and many will rejoice at his birth; for he will be great before the Lord, and he shall drink no wine or strong drink, and he will be filled with the Holy Spirit, even from his mother's womb. And he will turn many of the sons of Israel to the Lord their God, and he will go before him in the spirit and power of Elijah, to turn the hearts of the fathers to the children, and the disobedient to the wisdom of the just, to make ready for the Lord a people prepared.'

(As Elijah's mission was to prepare a penitent people, so John's mission is to turn the hearts of men from sin and towards the coming Messiah.)

Reflection

In our Advent themes the prophetic longings for the coming of the Messiah – God's visiting and redeeming his people – intermingle with the Church's longing for the final coming. Both hopes

are focused on and fulfilled in Jesus Christ. He is
God's Messiah, the coming one in whom God
takes our nature upon himself, where majesty is
seen in meekness and power in poverty. And as we
long for 'that promised time when war shall be no
more, oppression, lust and crime shall flee his face
before', when we glimpse something of the vision
of the Holy City, the New Jerusalem, and a time
when the 'kingdoms of this world become the
kingdom of our God and of his Christ, and he
shall reign for ever and ever', it is the same Christ
who came in humility for whom we long as the
Omega, the end of all things. As we have seen, the
Bible ends with the prayer of longing that Christ
will come and come quickly, for it is his redeeming
and transfiguring love which will judge and heal
and set to right the world's sorrow and pain.

The divine preparation of Elizabeth and
Zechariah for their task of bringing up what is, in
effect, the last of the Old Testament-style prophets
is meticulous. John will be filled with the Holy
Spirit. About him earlier prophets had made utterances. His task is two-fold – he both fulfils the
prophesies about him and closes the Old Testament by preparing and pointing men to the New
Adam of the New Testament.

The Offertory: *Ad te Domine*

Lead me forth in thy truth and teach me; for thou
art the God of my salvation; in thee hath been my
hope all the day long.

Mary:

Elizabeth told me about God's blessing on her and her conception of John. We discussed, almost without rest, how her son was to be filled with the Holy Spirit, and how his mission was to prepare for the coming of the promised Saviour. He would do this by making the people ready for the revelation of their Lord. Indeed, he would plainly point to the Lord. Neither of us then felt these to be odd concepts for our discussion: only a little earlier such things could not have been in our contemplation.

For further consideration . . .

Is my behaviour held to be the 'wisdom of the just'?

Day 19

The Book of the Prophet Isaiah 7 : 14

Therefore the Lord himself will give you a sign. Behold, a young woman shall conceive and bear a son, and shall call his name Immanuel.

The Gospel of Luke 1 : 26–38

In the sixth month the angel Gabriel was sent from God to a city of Galilee named Nazareth, to a virgin betrothed to a man whose name was Joseph, of the house of David; and the virgin's name was Mary. And he came to her and said, 'Hail, full of grace, the Lord is with you!' But she was greatly troubled at the saying, and considered in her mind what sort of greeting this might be. And the angel said to her, 'Do not be afraid, Mary, for you have found favour with God. And behold, you will conceive in your womb and bear a son, and you shall call his name Jesus. He will be great and will be called the Son of the Most High; and the Lord God will give to him the throne of his father David, and he will reign over the house of Jacob for ever; and of his kingdom there will be no end.'

And Mary said to the angel, 'How can this be, since I have no husband?' And the angel said to her, 'The Holy Spirit will come upon you, and the

power of the Most High will overshadow you;
therefore the child to be born will be called holy,
the Son of God. And behold, your kinswoman
Elizabeth in her old age has also conceived a son;
and this is the sixth month with her who was
called barren. For with God nothing will be
impossible.' And Mary said, 'Behold, I am the
handmaid of the Lord; let it be to me according to
your word.' And the angel departed from her.

(The child of Mary will be none other than God
with us.)

Reflection

To a village girl at Nazareth came the most overwhelming vocation, to be the mother of the Lord's
Anointed, the Christ of God, the very Son of God.
And Mary gave herself in trust and obedience, not
knowing how these things might be. As God prepared Jeremiah for his calling as a prophet, so he
prepared Mary for her calling as the Mother of his
Son. And that preparation and that calling is by
the Holy Spirit. When we think of the Virgin Birth
– or more properly, the virginal conception of
Jesus – we tend to think first of all of a physical
miracle, and that it most certainly is. But when the
Fathers of the Church spoke of the Virgin Birth,
they thought first and foremost of that miraculous
sign as a sign of the reality of God's New
Creation. God came to save his people, and save
them by becoming completely and wholly one of
them. New Creation – a creation animated by the

Holy Spirit of God – is at the heart of the Church's confession of the Virgin Birth of our Lord.

The Prophet Isaiah looked forward to God doing a 'new thing'. In and through the Blessed Virgin, that 'new thing' was done, but it was not done without human obedience and without human co-operation. If God's mighty work of salvation was to be achieved, if sin was to be conquered and the devil cast down, then the way of love of the God of Love was to seek the obedient and loving response of a young girl at Nazareth. Through her faith and obedience she became 'the gate of heaven's high Lord, the door through which the light has poured.' In her humility Mary is exalted, and in her we are given the pattern of faith, and an image of the Church.

The Sequence: *Verbum bonum et suave*

Sing we 'Ave' word endearing, Mary's welome, sweet and cheering, at the quickening salutation, David's seed of royal station won the Lord of all creation, Lily 'mid the thorns displayed.

Mary:

As you might expect, I was more than a little taken aback and astonished at the very presence of this messenger, this man (for so he appeared to me) let alone the subject of his announcement! However, he spoke with an irresistable *authority*. He disclosed in, perhaps, a rather matter-of-fact way, that he carried a message from Almighty

God himself – and I never doubted it. It was not in the least a later construction I placed upon the experience. Of course, the actual words he spoke I have mulled over time and time again. They are constantly in my mind. Every action of my son, every word and phrase, every nuance, is interpreted and reinterpreted in the light of those words. But I unequivocally accepted my part in God's plan, whatever that plan turned out to be. And the thought is as terrifying as it is exquisite.

I am here in the Temple having at last found my son. As he converses and disputes with the learned men, I ponder. The prophets of old not only suggest a wonderful future but also forsee rejection and suffering. Shall I cope?

For further consideration . . .

How clear is my 'Yes' to God?

Day 20

The Gospel of Luke 1 : 39–57

In those days Mary arose and went with haste into the hill country, to a city of Judah, and she entered the house of Zechariah and greeted Elizabeth. And when Elizabeth heard the greeting of Mary, the babe leaped in her womb; and Elizabeth was filled with the Holy Spirit and she exclaimed with a loud cry, 'Blessed are you among women, and blessed is the fruit of your womb! And why is this granted me, that the mother of my Lord should come to me? For behold, when the voice of your greeting came to my ears, the babe in my womb leaped for joy. And blessed is she who believed that there would be a fulfilment of what was spoken to her from the Lord.' And Mary said, 'My soul magnifies the Lord, and my spirit rejoices in God my Saviour, for he has regarded the low estate of his handmaiden. For behold, henceforth all generations will call me blessed; for he who is mighty has done great things for me, and holy is his name. And his mercy is on those who fear him from generation to generation. He has shown strength with his arm, he has scattered the proud in the imagination of their hearts, he has put down the mighty from their thrones, and exalted those of low degree; he has filled the hungry with good

*things, and the rich he has sent empty away. He
has helped his servant Israel, in remembrance of
his mercy, as he spoke to our fathers, to Abraham
and to his posterity for ever.'*

*And Mary remained with her about three
months, and returned to her home. Now the time
came for Elizabeth to be delivered, and she gave
birth to a son.*

(Although the template for this canticle would
seem to be Hannah's song (see Day 21), it is
clearly a modest cry from the heart of someone
who is steeped in the knowledge of Scripture. It is
a response to Elizabeth's congratulations.)

Reflection

'Blessed are you among women!' exclaims Elizabeth, 'and blessed is the fruit of your womb.' Luke
tells us of a moment of recognition not only by
Elizabeth but by the unborn John. This encounter
between the two mothers-to-be, each bearing a
child of promise and destiny, reminds us that what
we believe about the God who took our human
nature in Christ has important things to say about
unborn human life. Elizabeth, already six months
pregnant, recognizes her Saviour and her Lord
from the very point of conception. If Christians
have been concerned to revere unborn human life,
it is because we acknowledge conception as the
point from which a unique human life develops,
and because we believe that God himself took our
nature upon him from this very point. And it is

vital that we remain firm and steady in our reverence for the mystery of life: it is not something we are free to manipulate, destroy or experiment with for our own convenience or advantage.

As Christians we bear within ourselves the life and love of Christ, but a life and a love not yet made fully perfect. However, as Elizabeth recognized in Mary her very Saviour, so those we meet should be able to recognize in us something of the joy and the power of the life and love of Christ.

The Sequence: *Christi hodierna*

O Virgin, blessed of all generations; for thou alone wast worthy found to bear within thy womb him who bore all our sins.

Mary:

In heightened joy that was so much more than the everyday joy of life, I undertook the long journey from Nazareth to Jerusalem – a journey I was accustomed to – and then on to the hill country outside to visit my cousin, Elizabeth, who, the messenger had told me, was also to become a mother. As her pregnancy was more advanced than mine, I should gain from her experience.

Even her unborn child, she declared, seemed to sense the significance of my visit. We thanked God for his trust in us and thought, as I do now, about the titles lavished on the Anointed One, by the prophet Isaiah.

For further consideration . . .

Blessed means holy, favoured and content.

Day 21

The First Book of Samuel 2:1–11

Hannah also prayed and said, 'My heart exults in the Lord; my strength is exalted in the Lord. My mouth derides my enemies, because I rejoice in thy salvation. There is none holy like the Lord, there is none besides thee; there is no rock like our God. Talk no more so very proudly, let not arrogance come from my mouth; for the Lord is a God of knowledge, and by him actions are weighed. The bows of the mighty are broken, but the feeble gird on strength. Those who were full have hired them-selves out for bread, but those who were hungry have ceased to hunger. The barren has born seven, but she who has many children is forlorn. The Lord kills and brings to life; he brings down to Sheol and raises up. The Lord makes poor and makes rich; he brings low, he also exalts. He raises up the poor from the dust; he lifts the needy from the ash heap, to make them sit with princes and inherit a seat of honour. For the pillars of the earth are the Lord's, and on them he has set the world. He will guard the feet of his faithful ones; but the wicked shall be cut off in darkness; for not by might shall a man prevail. The adversaries of the Lord shall be broken to pieces; against them he will thunder in heaven. The Lord will judge the ends of the earth; he will give strength to his king, and exalt the power of his anointed.'

Then Elkanah went home to Ramah. And the boy [Samuel] ministered to the Lord, in the presence of Eli the priest.

(Hannah's circumstances were similar to Elizabeth's but Luke rightly places the Magnificat upon the lips of Mary. Mary is content to remain a slave of the Lord.)

Reflection

As if to underline our longing for the coming of the Saviour, and the fact that the Feast of the Nativity is now not far away, the Church has for many centuries prescribed a series of antiphons to be recited before and after the Magnificat at the evening office. These 'Great O' antiphons are cries from the heart expressing an earnest yearning for Christ. In temperament they contrast with the text of the Magnificat itself but complement it. The hymn, recorded only in the Gospel of Luke, was sung by Mary at her Visitation with Elizabeth, when the birth of Jesus was still nine months away and, perhaps, the yearning 'O' not far from her lips.

Mary gave herself in love to God's service with this response to Gabriel's Annunciation: 'Behold, I am the handmaid of the Lord; let it be to me according to thy word.' After only a few days Mary is with Elizabeth and in joy cries out: 'He who is mighty has done great things for me.' It is a hymn about God's doing what we least expect; about how he can turn our values and certainties upside down. It is a song sung in humility, and reflects the Song of the Hannah, the mother of Samuel.

The 'O' of each antiphon sums up the longing of Israel for the Messiah and for redemption, and consequently our longing that we may ourselves reveal something of the life and love of Christ.

The Antiphon: O *Sapientia*

O Wisdom, thou camest from the mouth of the Most High, and reachest mightily from one end to the other ordering all things with sweetness. Come and instruct us in the way of prudence.

Mary:

I remember that my song of thanksgiving reflected Hannah's own song: it was such a prayerful song. Hannah and Elizabeth shared much. Both had conceived in old age; both sons would execute God's special mission: the first anointed the son of Jesse for kingship, and the second will point to the man chosen to shoulder the responsibility of David and make a kingdom for God.

These thoughts arise naturally and constantly from the words of God's own messenger who spoke to Zechariah and to me.

For further consideration . . .

How deep is my longing to reveal something of the love of Christ?

Glory to God

Day 22

The Gospel of Luke 3 : 2b–6, 15, 16

The word of God came to John the son of Zechariah in the wilderness and he went into all the region about the Jordan, preaching a baptism of repentance for the forgiveness of sins. As it is written in the book of the words of Isaiah the prophet, 'The voice of one crying in the wilderness: Prepare the way of the Lord, make his paths straight. Every valley shall be filled, and every mountain and hill shall be brought low, and the crooked shall be made straight, and the rough ways shall be made smooth; and all flesh shall see the salvation of God.'

As the people were in expectation, and all men questioned in their hearts concerning John, whether perhaps he were the Christ, John answered them all, 'I baptize you with water; but he who is mightier than I is coming, the thong of whose sandals I am not worthy to untie; he will baptize with the Holy Spirit and with fire.'

(John was preparing the way at many levels, for example, within the above passage (vv. 10–14) he anticipates in his generosity to soldiers and publicans the teaching of Jesus.)

Reflection

In the days of John, the country was troubled, as it is today. It was subject to a foreign power; there was corruption and oppression. There was much questioning about why God allowed the situation to be as it was. There were revolutionaries anxious to take up arms. There were others, those who wrote the so-called Dead Sea Scrolls, who said that as it was a wicked world it was better to withdraw and await the Messiah. There were Sadducees anxious to get on with the Roman authorities; and there were Pharisees anxious that everyone should return to a strict observance of the letter of the law. Out of the fog of this confusion of ideas emerged John the Baptist, a wild kind of character living off an unappetizing diet and wearing animal skins – a character not obviously at home with any of the above. It is he who, in a living summary of all the prophets before him, prepares the world by baptism in the Jordan, urging the people first to repent and make themselves ready for the Christ who will come 'baptizing with the Holy Spirit and with fire.'

Our preparation in penitence is also an essential part of our being ready to meet the new-born Christ in the simplicity of the stable.

The Antiphon: *O Adonai*

O Adonai, and Head of the house of Israel, who appearedst in the bush to Moses in a flame of fire, and gavest him the law of Sinai: come and deliver us with an outstretched arm.

Mary:

And how shall John prepare the people and point the way to my son? Isaiah certainly spoke of such a forerunner if we understand him correctly. How does this make sense of the descriptions of the Anointed One? That one man can prepare for another I can understand: what I do not yet understand is why we hear in other passages that the Anointed One, the Messiah, must suffer.

For further consideration . . .

Am I yet ready to meet the new-born Christ?

Day 23

The Gospel of John 1:1–9,14,15

In the beginning was the Word, and the Word was with God, and the Word was God. He was in the beginning with God, all things were made through him, and without him was not made anything that was made. In him was life, and the life was the light of men. The light shines in the darkness, and the darkness has not overcome it.

There was a man sent from God, whose name was John. He came for testimony, to bear witness to the light, that all might believe through him. He was not the light, but came to bear witness to the light. The true light that enlightens every man was coming into the world.

And the Word became flesh and dwelt among us, full of grace and truth; we have beheld his glory, glory as of the only Son from the Father.

John bore witness to him, and cried, 'This was he of whom I said, "he who comes after me ranks before me, for he was before me."'

(John the Baptist, the Apostles and the Church bear witness to the Divinity of Jesus.)

Reflection

For the author of the Gospel of John, the good news of the coming of Jesus Christ is expressed not in a nativity story but in the mysterious though powerful language of the Word of God becoming flesh. The Word is God's expression and self-communication. In the Old Testament God's will and purpose are made known by his Word, which comes to the prophets. In the writings we know as the 'Wisdom' literature of the Hebrew Scriptures, the Wisdom of God is seen as the agent of God in creation; and in Greek thought, the Divine Reason holds the world together, and is its meaning, order and purpose. Hebrew and Greek thought conjoin in the Word, which John's Gospel proclaims was 'with God and was God'.

The coming of Jesus is new creation, as we have seen in the fundamental meaning of the virginal conception of Jesus in the Gospels of Matthew and Luke. It is here expressed in another way with the words 'in the beginning' echoing the opening words of the creation story in the first chapter of Genesis. The God who is the origin of all things acts in a new way to redeem creation by an act of new creation. The Word, God's own communication and expression of his being, becomes flesh and, therefore, the creator knows his creation from the inside.

'We beheld his glory' in the weakness of a new-born baby, and John then balances the picture of this humble descent into humanity perfectly, in his recollection of the Last Supper towards the end of his Gospel, he records that Jesus' prelude to the washing of the disciples' feet was the 'laying aside of his garments'. The glory of God's redeeming love is known in a child in Bethlehem, in the menial duties of a servant, and, in the end, in arms outstretched and nailed to a cross in the embrace of love.

The Antiphon: *O Radix Jesse*

O Root of Jesse, which standest for an ensign of the people, at whom kings shall close their mouths, to whom the Gentiles shall come: come and deliver us, and wait not.

Mary:

I do believe that God's plan is unfolded for us in the history of his chosen people and through his prophets; and I accept without demur my humble part in it. My son will be – and Simeon spoke of this – a light that will enlighten the whole of mankind.

For further consideration . . .

Jesus said: 'Before Abraham was, I am.'

Day 24

The Gospel of Mark 1:2–8

As it is written in Isaiah the prophet, 'Behold, I send my messenger before thy face, who shall prepare the way; the voice of one crying in the wilderness: Prepare the way of the Lord, make his paths straight.'

John the baptizer appeared in the wilderness, preaching a baptism of repentance for the forgiveness of sins. And there went out to him all the country of Judea, and all the people of Jerusalem; and they were baptized by him in the river Jordan, confessing their sins. Now John was clothed with camel's hair, and had a leather girdle around his waist, and ate locusts and wild honey. And he preached, saying, 'After me comes he who is mightier than I, the thong of whose sandals I am not worthy to stoop down and untie. I have baptized you with water; but he will baptize you with the Holy Spirit.'

(The quotation is from the Prophet Malachi rather than Isaiah and this imagery is drawn from the custom of the sending of a herald to warn of the visit of the king, so that, literally, any potholes and obstructions in the roadway can be made good in advance.)

Reflection

To be baptized marks a fresh start. First, a disappearance beneath the surface of the water and then emergence into new life, to a new commitment to God. The crowds who came to be baptized came in search of new life. To be baptized by John was to turn from sin. Surely there would be no need for Jesus to be baptized.

But how else would John recognize Jesus in order to point him out? Would the Holy Spirit identify him? Perhaps he was already known to John by reputation? Was he already known to John through family ties? After all, their mothers had shared much. And how do we recognize Jesus and in what and in whom can we recognize him? His presence is truly in the most holy sacrament of the altar and we recognize him as certainly as the disciples recognized him after the walk to Emmaus. He is in the Word and he is there in the glory of others and is plain to see. But do we recognize him in the less obvious places – in the needs of the poor and lonely, the deprived and the sick? If we fail to respond to them in their need when the opportunity arises, we fail to recognize Jesus and our sins of omission against those less fortunate than ourselves are sins of omission against our Lord himself.

The Antiphon: *O Clavis David*

O Key of David, and Sceptre of the house of Israel; that openest and man shutteth not, that shuttest and man openeth not. Come and bring the prisoner out of gaol, and the man that sitteth in darkness and in the shadow of death.

Mary:

John's immense duty, then, will be to turn God's people towards the coming Messiah. (Do I know that my 'Son of the Most High' is indeed that Messiah? Yes, I am sure.) John will wake up the children of Israel as did the prophets of old, except that he will cry 'It is now! Here he is!'

For further consideration . . .

Am I unworthy to stoop down to untie the thong of those sandals?

Day 25

The Gospel of Matthew 1 : 18–23

Now the birth of Jesus Christ took place in this way. When his mother Mary had been betrothed to Joseph, before they came together she was found to be with child of the Holy Spirit; and her husband, Joseph, being a just man and unwilling to put her to shame, resolved to send her away quietly. But as he considered this, behold, an angel of the Lord appeared to him in a dream, saying, 'Joseph, son of David, do not fear to take Mary your wife, for that which is conceived in her is of the Holy Spirit; she will bear a son, and you shall call his name Jesus, for he will save his people from their sins.' All this took place to fulfil what the Lord had spoken by the prophet: 'Behold, a virgin shall conceive and bear a son, and his name shall be called Emmanuel.'

(According to Jewish law the status of husband and wife was conferred upon a couple at betrothal. A child conceived during this time was taken to be legitimate unless it was disowned. The marriage was complete only after the husband had taken his bride to his own home.)

Reflection

Mary's 'yes' – her positive response to her vocation
– was what God required for our salvation. For
God never imposes, he always asks us for our co-
operation, our response of faith, even faith as tiny
as a grain of mustard seed. Luke gives us many
accounts which may well have come from the lips
of Mary herself. Joseph, on the other hand, is
Matthew's concern in his birth narrative and here
Joseph is anxious about Mary's reputation and, as
a man of honour, decides to divorce her infor-
mally. But then, in a dream, the angel tells Joseph
that the child to which Mary is to give birth is a
child of promise, conceived by the creative Spirit of
God. The child is to be given the name Jesus – the
one who saves. The prophet's words are cited and
we are reminded that the promised child will be
nothing other than 'God with us'.

As Paul puts it so powerfully in his Letter to the
Philippians, God 'emptied himself' and gave himself fully into our human condition and then, as
John says at the beginning of his Gospel, he 'dwelt
among us' – literally, he 'pitched his tent among
us'.

The Antiphon: *O Oriens*

O Dayspring, Brilliance of Light eternal, and Sun
of Righteousness. Come and enlighten him that
sitteth in darkness and in the shadow of death.

Mary:

Joseph was disturbed and shaken at the state of affairs occasioned by the announcement to me. He was, however, comforted by the revelation he himself received to allay his fears, and he prepared for his work as guardian with gentle enthusiasm.

For further consideration . . .

The 'God with us' of Emmanuel is, of course, the 'God with us' of Christ.

Day 26

The Gospel of Luke 2 : 1,3 – 5

In those days a decree went out from Caesar Augustus that all the world should be enrolled. And all went to be enrolled, each to his own city. And Joseph also went up from Galilee, from the city of Nazareth, to Judea, to the city of David, which is called Bethlehem, because he was of the house and lineage of David, to be enrolled with Mary his betrothed, who was with child.

(Augustus had instigated similar tax censuses in Gaul in 12 BC and in Egypt in 10–9 BC.)

Reflection

Luke sets the scene with precision and identifies the rather mundane reason for the couple's journey to Bethlehem. This is firmly down-to-earth and contrasts dramatically with the extravagant scenes artists through the ages have drawn from Luke's account of the birth. But these familiar Christmas stories found in the Gospels of Matthew and Luke are stories told, as is the case with the Gospels as a whole, in the light of Easter. Without Easter no one would have thought to set down these stories, or to find any good news at all in the child born at Bethlehem. The stories of the birth of Jesus are, paradoxically, Easter stories; for it is in the light of Easter that we see what God has done in and through the child whose birth we are preparing to celebrate. Christmas is new life born in a cave, foreshadowing the new life to be born in the grave at Easter.

The Antiphon: *O Rex gentium*

O King of the nations, and their Desire, the Cornerstone who makest both one. Come and save mankind whom thou formedst of earth.

Mary:

I constantly question myself: did I properly understand the messenger in the first place? I am sure that I did. I store and add to my developing knowledge even the things that seem to be of little moment, but I cannot now be more sure of the vocation I freely accepted.

I stayed with Elizabeth until she was due to give birth to John.

By my return to Nazareth, Joseph had become convinced of the meaning of the annunciation to me.

Months later, we were travelling together that well-trodden road to Jerusalem. We were responding to the insistence of the Roman authorities that every man should register at the census station in the city of his birth, or of his family. In Joseph's case, that place was Bethlehem, David's own city.

For further consideration . . .

The poet Gerard Manley Hopkins spoke about Christ 'Eastering' in us. Does he 'Easter' in me?

Day 27

The Gospel of Matthew 2:1–6

Now when Jesus was born in Bethlehem of Judea in the days of Herod the king, behold, wise men from the East came to Jerusalem, saying, 'Where is he who has been born king of the Jews? For we have seen his star in the East, and have come to worship him.' When Herod the king heard this, he was troubled, and all Jerusalem with him; and assembling all the chief priests and scribes of the people, he inquired of them where the Christ was to be born. They told him, 'In Bethlehem of Judea; for so it is written by the prophets: "And you, O Bethlehem, in the land of Judah, are by no means least among the rulers of Judah; for from you shall come a ruler who will govern my people Israel."'

(The Magi clearly came from somewhere east of the Jordan and Dead Sea. The sight of a particular star in the eastern sky causes them to travel west to the Jewish capital for further evidence of their quest.)

Reflection

'If the Christ is to be born in Bethlehem as predicted by the prophet, it will upset the accommodation we have with the Romans, and my position as king, sanctioned and protected by the Romans, will be much weakened.' So Herod the Great would have reasoned as he paced up and down in his palace. 'I'll consult my experts in these matters first, then decide how to proceed without alarming the foreigners.'

The dreadful news that a longed-for prophecy might be about to be realized was certainly going to be inconvenient, to say the least. Indeed, at its worst, it would turn the world upside down!

Of course, that is just what the coming of Christ did. It was never going to be 'convenient'. It most certainly was not 'convenient' for Mary but her response to God was simply 'yes'. And Mary went further, glorying in the fact that God was a God who was able to turn man's world upside down, and who did the things least expected.

The Antiphon: *O Emmanuel*

O Emmanuel, our King and Giver of Law, the Desire of nations, and their salvation. Come and save us, O Lord God.

Mary:

When we saw that camel train in Jerusalem forty days after the birth, we wondered about the destination and the aim of the principal parties.

Later, we were to realize that they had been enquiring, perhaps of King Herod himself, the whereabouts of Bethlehem and its significance.

Would God inform foreign kings of the birth of

the 'Son of the Most High' by setting a particularly brilliant star in the heavens? Indeed!

For further consideration . . .

To what extent is my Herodness apparent?

Day 28

(24 December – The Eve of the Nativity)

The Gospel of Luke 2:6–14

And while they were there, the time came for her to be delivered. And she gave birth to her first-born son and wrapped him in swaddling cloths, and laid him in a manger, because there was no place for them in the inn.

And in that region there were shepherds out in the field, keeping watch over their flock by night. And an angel of the Lord appeared to them, and the glory of the Lord shone around them, and they were filled with fear. And the angel said to them, 'Be not afraid; for behold, I bring you good news of great joy which will come to all the people; for to you is born this day in the city of David a Saviour, who is Christ the Lord. And this will be a sign for you: you will find a babe wrapped in swaddling cloths and lying in a manger.' And suddenly there was with the angel a multitude of the heavenly host praising God and saying, 'Glory to God in the highest, and on earth peace among men with whom he is pleased!'

(The translation of the cry of the heavenly host has often been accompanied by controversy. The angel tells the shepherds that the joy is for 'all people'. If for all, the 'peace among men' would seem to be peace among those who have become the object of this generosity – i.e. humanity generally.)

Reflection

The shepherds, as Luke portrays them, glimpsed the radiance of God's glory in a vision of the angelic praise of heaven, an experience which was for them both wonderful and overwhelming. But that vision was not, and could not be, for them the end of the matter. They had to act in response to what they had seen. In the Acts of the Apostles we are told how Paul, making his defence against King Agrippa, spoke of his vision on the Damascus road, and how his life from that point was changed because he could not be disobedient to the heavenly vision. So the shepherds were driven by what they had seen, by that moment of revelation and that glimpse of God's glory, to go to find God in the ordinary life of their local town.

All too often we tend to doubt the reality and comprehensiveness of God's love. It is easier to 'domesticate' God's love and make faith our hobby than to risk ourselves in discovering its true dimensions. It is as if the shepherds had, instead of going to Bethlehem, continued to sit on the hillside with their sheep, talking of the wonderful experience that they had had, and trying to make it happen again.

The shepherds did not fail to respond to their vision.

The Sequence: *Nato canunt omnia*

All hosts, above, beneath, sing the incarnate Lord,
with instruments and pious breath attune each
measured word.
'Glory to God on high' on this renowned night
was thundered forth in harmony by angel legions
bright.

Mary:

We arrived outside an inn on that strangest of
nights. I was about to give birth and clearly could
travel no farther. The wife of the innkeeper –
already in a high state of excitement over their
crowded establishment – generously accommo-
dated us away from the cold night air, and
assumed the rôle of an efficient midwife. A dog
barked and sheep and goats bleated, then fell
silent as if giving way to the sound of joy and
happiness bursting out of heaven, and filling the
world for all time. Such was my frame of mind.
The word of God had been realized.

I was anxious that my good friend should not
neglect her guests but she would insist on my taking food and drink, as is the way of generous
innkeepers' wives. Her name was Miriam.

There was a fleeting moment of disquiet when
I saw the ominous shape of a cross projected on
the ceiling by the flickering oil lamp through the
cross-members of the sheep's manger we had
utilized for a bed for the child. This image would
be summoned again by Simeon a few weeks later,

and it is occasionally conjured up for no apparent reason in my mind's eye.

For further consideration . . .

How readily do I ignore the visions I have been granted?

In a Manger

Day 29

(25 December – The Nativity of Our Lord)

The Gospel of Luke 2:15–20

When the angels went away from them into heaven, the shepherds said to one another, 'Let us go over to Bethlehem and see this thing that has happened, which the Lord has made known to us.' And they went with haste, and found Mary and Joseph, and the babe lying in a manger. And when they saw it they made known the saying which had been told them concerning this child; and all who heard it wondered at what the shepherds told them. But Mary kept all these things in her heart. And the shepherds returned, glorifying and praising God for all they had heard and seen, as it had been told them.

(The shepherds here are representative of the whole of Israel. The Word was made known to them. Bethlehem was renowned for its sheep and, consequently, for its shepherds. But these shepherds were, in many respects, outsiders, in view of their inability to observe strictly the laws of their religion on account of their mode of life.)

Reflection

Because the glory the shepherds had seen and the God they sought was love, they only fully understood the splendour that had shone round about them when they saw it in the weakness and simplicity of a new-born child, whose only resting-place was a feeding trough roughly made, perhaps, from unplaned, sawn timber. And it was from this point that they returned glorifying and praising God.

To know that God has known our common life, the ordinariness of being man; to know that he has known the weakness and fear, and the need for love; is to know that nobody can force us into a situation which is beyond the range of God's love and concern, and that there are no circumstances which cannot be irradiated by his glory if we look upon them with the eyes of his love.

As countless Christians have discovered through the centuries, it is because God wishes to draw us to himself, and intends us to discover his reality and his love in the world and in all areas of our lives, that he will not allow us to rest in any selfish enjoyment of the vision that first fired us. Like the shepherds, we may discover that instead of or in addition to the vision of angels, we have been given the gift of God himself.

The Sequence: *Nato canunt omnia*

This is the hallowed morn when on our fallen race in full effulgence rose the dawn of new-born joy and grace.

Amazing splendours shone – a strange unwonted sight – upon the shepherds biding lone under the veil of night.

Mary:

So my task began. The 'Son of the Most High' would be suckled at my breast and nurtured in my own home. How might he be the cause of pain; how might he suffer it? I still wonder, but that natal night held little for me other than unalloyed joy. Miriam eventually left me for other duties while Joseph, much pleased as guardian of the precious swaddled child, returned to the broken treadle-lathe he had been repairing, knowing his immediate presence inappropriate.

A little later, this curious spectacle was observed by shepherd boys who could utter nothing other than 'cor!' The 'Son of the Most High' worshipped and adored in a single syllable – and that said it all.

For further consideration . . .

How shall I spread the joy of the angels this Christmas?

Day 30

The Gospel of Matthew 2 : 7, 8

Then Herod summoned the wise men secretly and ascertained from them what time the star appeared; and he sent them to Bethlehem, saying, 'Go and search diligently for the child, and when you have found him bring me word, that I too may come and worship him.'

(Herod is, presumably, calculating the age of the child by taking the first reported appearance of the star as an indication of the time of the birth.)

Reflection

Matthew gives us the story of Herod and the Wise Men in some detail.

Herod summoned the Wise Men 'secretly', out of the hearing, presumably, of his scribes and advisers. 'Yes, I can help you by pointing you in the right direction, but please repay this effort by reporting to me after you have found this child. I should also like to visit him and worship him myself.' Might Herod have whispered to himself when the Wise Men had turned their backs 'for it expedient that one should die for the people' in an anticipation of the words of Caiaphas?

Herod was a strong man of action; one who

would not be thwarted, tricked or deceived. If he were, the consequences would be even more terrible. This reminds us that both Jesus and the gospel belong to the harsh reality of our fallen world. We are involved not in a fantastic dream or sentimental tale, but in a faith springing from a life lived out in an oppressive and violent moment of human history.

The Sequence: *Nato canunt omnia*

Who was before all time is born of purest Maid; Glory to God in heights sublime, peace comes the world to aid.
Even thus the choir on high sings praises jubilant, from pole to pole their voices fly, heaven echoes to their chant.

Mary:

What would King Herod have asked of or told the travellers? In a seemingly friendly exchange they must have disclosed the nature of their mission to Herod. What then began to brew deep within him? How could the birth of something holy produce such evil?

For further consideration . . .

May I never worship the Christ-Child with the sword of division concealed in my heart.

Day 31

The Gospel of Luke 2 : 21

And at the end of eight days, when he was circumcised, he was called Jesus, the name given by the angel before he was conceived in the womb.

(Now confirmed in the circumcision rite, Jesus is the heir of the promise made to Abraham.)

Reflection

Dutifully, and in accordance with the law, Joseph and Mary ensured that at the prescribed time our Lord was circumcised, and named Jesus, as the angel had decreed in his Annunciation to Mary and in Joseph's vision. And further, after forty days from the birth, purifying sacrifices had to be offered in the Temple, and the child presented. They go to the Temple to perform a ritual, to stand again, according to the law of Moses, in a right relationship with God and with his people. But what they are pointed to is a purification which goes far beyond the law of Moses; to a hope of a new relationship with God, which is the fulfilment of the longings of the prophets; to God's giving of himself to mankind. To know that kind of purification may well be painful; for it is the purification that springs from coming to know the reality of the love of God, and being receptive to that power of loving in every part of our being. And that love of God is not to be trifled with, as though it were merely the assurance of a sentimental benevolence indulging our every wish. The love in question is rather to be compared to the fire by which silver is refined (as the Prophet Malachi suggests); it is a love that is creative and renewing. It is a demanding love that through us God may reach out into the world to heal and to save; to love all people into their full humanity.

The Sequence: *Eia recolamus*

Let us devoutly pay with joy and praises meet, our reverence to this holy day, which dawns with radiance sweet.
Darkness hath passed away, the mist of night retires, the daystar of the sea today with health the world inspires.

Mary:

In a day or so, Joseph settled us into the home of a relative, and soon afterwards the child was named Jesus. There we stayed until after we had made the journey to Jerusalem to perform the ceremonies of the purification and presentation, though we were already making plans either for settling in the area or for a return to Nazareth. In either place Joseph would be much needed for his woodworking expertise.

Rumours reigned in Jerusalem about those

camels stationed close to Herod's palace. Apparently, even by his standards, they were an unusual sight. On our return to Bethlehem, Joseph cited a passage of Isaiah that referred to 'dromedaries of Midian and Ephah' and a psalm that brought to mind the spectacle.

For further consideration . . .

As our Lord sheds blood for the first time, we think of the final lance-thrust to his heart. Do my words and deeds ever pierce his heart?

Day 32

The Gospel of Matthew 2 : 9, 10

When they had heard the king they went their way; and lo, the star which they had seen in the East went before them, till it came to rest over the place where the child was. When they saw the star they rejoiced exceedingly with great joy.

(They see the star again and, armed with knowledge of the road to Bethlehem received from Herod's court, they proceed.)

Reflection

After they have secretly discussed their quest with Herod, and bowed to his wishes regarding the child, the Wise Men emerge from the palace by which the star has been temporarily obscured from their view. They are glad to see it poised over the town to which they have been given directions. What is in their minds? They have not had the advantage of the vision lavished upon the shepherds. Theirs has been a dogged and painstaking seeking after the truth, aided by the conjuctions of the stars and positions of the heavenly bodies. As their camels swagger towards Bethlehem, they pause from discussion and consider in their minds' eyes what might have been the local effect of so important a birth. Something drives them on. Do they know that the child will be 'God with us'? Have they read the Jewish prophets as well as the stars? Do they know that they represent the whole of the Gentile world as they advance towards Bethlehem to see the love that has been born in a stable?

The Sequence: *Epiphaniam Domino*

Now the choir their voice unite, organs swell with mystic rite, bringing to the King of kings, praise and costly offerings.
O'er all kingdoms, o'er all lands may he spread his sheltering hands ever present to defend, unto worlds that never end.

Mary:

I remember that the travellers told Joseph's brother-in-law (in whose house we were living), that the star they had used for guidance beamed with an even finer precision to lead them to their destination, after their audience with Herod.

For further consideration . . .

The wise men rejoiced. Their vision was clear; their aim was clear.

Day 33

Psalm 72 [71]:1-4, 10-15a, 19

Give the king thy justice, O God, and thy right-
eousness to the royal son! May he judge thy
people with righteousness, and the poor with
justice! Let the mountains bear prosperity for the
people, and the hills, in righteousness! May he
defend the cause of the poor of the people, give
deliverance to the needy, and crush the oppressor!
May the kings of Tarshish and of the isles render
him tribute, may the kings of Sheba and Seba
bring gifts! May all kings fall down before him, all
nations serve him! For he delivers the needy when
he calls, the poor and him who has no helper. He
has pity on the weak and the needy, and saves the
lives of the needy. From oppression and violence
he redeems their life; and precious is their blood in
his sight. Long may he live, may gold of Sheba be
given to him! Blessed be his glorious name for
ever; may his glory fill the whole earth!

(This psalm sings of the characteristics of an ideal
king, which can be fulfilled only with the coming
of the Messiah. In the light of Christ's birth we see
it as a profoundly prophetic psalm.)

Reflection

We know from Luke and Matthew the effect of the birth on the representatives of ordinary Jewish folk, and on the Wise Men. How might the moment of the birth of the Word-made-flesh have seemed or been recalled, say, by Joseph? After all, it was a new beginning; things had changed. It was evidence of a new creation.

In one of the early Christian writings, the Protevangelion of James, the narratives of the birth and infancy are elaborated. There is a moving passage (Chapter 13), which speaks of the whole of creation catching its breath. The words are put into the mouth of Joseph, who is looking for a midwife to help Mary in her labour.

Now I, Joseph, was walking, yet I walked not. I looked up into the air and gazed in amazement. And I looked up unto the pole of heaven and saw it standing still, and saw that the birds of the heavens were without motion. And I looked upon the earth and saw a bowl set, and workmen lying beside it with their hands in the bowl: and those who were chewing, chewed not, and those who were lifting the food, lifted not, and those who put it to their mouths, put it not thereto. But the faces of all of them were looking upward. And, behold, there were sheep being driven, and they went not forward but stood still; and the shepherd lifted his hand to urge them with his staff, and his hand remained there. And I looked upon the stream of the river, and saw the mouths of the kids upon the

water that they drank not. And of a sudden, all
things moved onward in their natural course.

All things hold their breath, all are caught in a
moment of wonder when God comes among us.

The Sequence: *Sonent regi nato*

O Wonderful, mysterious generation! O most
astonishing nativity!
O glorious child! O Deity incarnate! So had the
prophets, by the Spirit moved, declared thou
should'st be born, thou Son of God!
The face of all the elements is gladdened, and all
the saints exultingly rejoice, crying 'All hail!'

Mary:

Even the Psalms of Kings David and Solomon took
on fresh prophetic meaning as we later discussed
the extraordinary visitation by representatives of
monarchs and potentates in far-distant lands of the
pagan world. It is so clear that the privilege of
God's chosen people is to enlighten the world by
showing God's work in its history and now by
revealing to it the promised Saviour of all mankind. I wonder, though, how this will be achieved
in my son. Certainly, there is no doubting his ability as he continues to examine the elders with his
precocious penetrating enquiry.

For further consideration . . .

Do I take time to ponder the works of God and to admire his handiwork?

Day 34

The Gospel of Matthew 2 : 11, 12

And going into the house they saw the child with Mary his mother, and fell down and worshipped him. Then, opening their treasures, they offered him gifts, gold, frankincense and myrrh. And being warned in a dream not to return to Herod, they departed to their own country by another way.

(The offering of frankincense – *precious* incense – was usually reserved for the divine even in 'pagan' races. The gifts were clearly products of the Magi's native lands.)

Reflection

Matthew's account of the birth of Jesus has the story of the Wise Men at its centre. It is a story that was seen as the manifestation of Christ to the Gentiles, the acknowledgement by the Gentile world of the Lord's Anointed, the promised Messiah of the Jewish people. A star leads them to Jerusalem, and then, pointed onwards by Herod and the Jewish scholars, to Bethlehem, the City of David. They enter the house over which the star appears to stand, and prostrate themselves in worship, presenting gifts of gold, frankincense and myrrh.

The earliest Christian interpretation of this familiar Epiphany story was not so much the coming of the Gentiles to adore the Christ-Child, but a sign of the Lordship of Christ over the dark powers and forces of the universe. The Wise Men, the Magi, were both astronomers and astrologers – star-gazers in the widest sense – reading the fate of the world in their calculations. Their bowing down in worship of the child, having been led there by those very stars, was a sign that Christ was the Lord of the heavens; that the child Jesus was the one who ruled the universe. But he, the Lord of the Universe, comes down to our level. He is the child on Mary's knee, and his Lordship and his power are the ingredients of a love that gives itself away and empties itself into the powerlessness of a little child.

The Sequence: *Epiphaniam Domino*

Him their costly offering, Gold, myrrh, incense, wise men bring.
God, sweet incense; precious gold a king; myrrh doth a man unfold.

Mary:

But on the night those outlandish caravans found their way to the house in Bethlehem and looked for my new-born son, I had little time to allow my mind free reign. With flounces of colourful finery, they left over-generous gifts of gold, frankincense, and myrrh. We understood that the three travellers had been alerted independently in their several lands to the true meaning of the star and to Bethlehem.

I am sure that any further significance to be found in those gifts will later be revealed to me when God's plan is uncovered but I do know, as I knew then, that gold signifies kingship; incense, divinity and holiness; myrrh, mortality.

For further consideration . . .

If grand, wealthy men, at home in the courts and palaces of foreign kings, can bow down before a child . . .

Day 35

The Gospel of Luke 2 : 22, 24–35

*And when they came for their purification accord-
ing to the law of Moses, they brought him up to
Jerusalem to present him to the Lord and to offer
a sacrifice according to what is said in the law of
the Lord, 'a pair of turtledoves or two young
pigeons'. Now there was a man in Jerusalem,
whose name was Simeon, and this man was righteous and devout, looking for the consolation of
Israel, and the Holy Spirit was upon him. And it
was revealed to him by the Holy Spirit that he
should not see death before he had seen the Lord's
Christ. And inspired by the Spirit he came into the
temple; and when the parents brought in the child
Jesus, to do for him according to the custom of the
law, he took him up in his arms and said, 'Lord,
now lettest thou thy servant depart in peace,
according to thy word; for mine eyes have seen thy
salvation which thou hast prepared in the presence
of all peoples, a light for revelation to the
Gentiles, and for glory to thy people Israel.'*

*And his father and his mother marvelled at
what was said about him; and Simeon blessed
them and said to Mary his mother, 'Behold, this
child is set for the fall and rising of many in Israel,
and for a sign that is spoken against (and a sword*

will pierce through your own soul also), that
thoughts out of many hearts will be revealed.'

('Their' purification suggests that Luke is thinking
of the Levitical ceremony of presentation and
redemption as, under the law, neither Jesus nor
Joseph would have required purification. There
was, in fact, no requirement for a woman to make
a special journey to the Temple for purification.)

Reflection

At the end of his birth narrative, Luke records in a
simple note that 'Mary kept all these things
and pondered them in her heart'. Here, Luke is
saying to us something so surpassingly wonderful
that we need to return to contemplate it time
and time again: that Mary, the Virgin Mother of
God, is said to 'keep and ponder'. She treasures
them up and she meditates, reflects, and engages
deeply with their meaning. The Greek word we
translate as 'ponder' means really 'to symbolize'
and almost 'to kindle the imagination' about
something, and even, if we pushed it a little further, 'to be set on fire' about something. This tells
us something important about Christian prayer.
The old medieval monks were said to 'ruminate'
on Scripture, 'to chew it over' as a ruminant chews
the cud. So many Christians think of prayer
simply as asking God for things; that is only a
small part of prayer. When we pray deeply we
should be like those old monks, chewing over the
words of Scripture; or, better still, like Mary,

kindling our imaginations and pondering in our hearts. Then we shall be able to say with Simeon 'For I have seen with my own eyes your promised salvation, a salvation you have prepared for all to see'.

The Sequence: *Celeste organum*

Lo! earth is joined with things divine, in this respect their lays combine.
O man, rejoice, and ponder this accord; O flesh, rejoice, combining with the Word.
Star of the sea! Thy blessed Son the holy Church adores.

Mary:

I sit here in contemplation. Gabriel spoke about the nature of my son and this accords with the utterances of the prophets. I associated the two immediately but then began to consider carefully other, less grand sayings – the sayings about rejection and suffering I have already mentioned a number of times. I still find this aspect difficult to fathom, but my commission is simply to bring up my son.

My concern over what lay in the future was reinforced and almost put into words in this very building after I had presented Jesus and after a purifying sacrifice had been made forty days after childbirth. We had ridden here from Bethlehem. After the ceremony, the venerable Simeon took Jesus in his arms and spoke enigmatically for a moment or two, then directed his fading, whitened eyes to me and predicted distress, sharp pain and sorrow.

For further consideration . . .

We present ourselves and are purified through absolution and then, like Simeon, we receive the Lord.

Out of Egypt

THE JOYFUL MYSTERIES
IV· The Presentation in the Temple

Day 36

The Gospel of Matthew 2 : 13, 14

Now when they had departed, behold, an angel of the Lord appeared to Joseph in a dream and said, 'Rise, take the child and his mother, and flee to Egypt, and remain there till I tell you; for Herod is about to search for the child, to destroy him.' And he rose and took the child and his mother by night, and departed to Egypt.

(Such a journey would have taken about six days. Egypt was a traditional place of refuge. At the time there was a significant Jewish population in Alexandria and Heliopolis.)

Reflection

The Wise Men adore the child, as do the shepherds in Luke's Gospel. But then danger strikes and Matthew tells how Joseph is made to realize that he must flee to Egypt with Mary and the infant Jesus, away from Herod's jurisdiction. This profoundly important decision is made by Joseph as guardian of the child Jesus. He manifests his quiet authority over the situation and in more than an echo of the settling in Egypt in the time of Jacob and Joseph, he takes Mary and the child away, by night, from the danger of the impending massacre.

Perhaps we treat this story lightly, but if you are a Christian in Egypt, you would never think of this story as a minor incident. In the Coptic Church, the ancient Church of Egypt, the flight into Egypt is very important. Go to a rather scruffy suburb of Cairo and you will be shown a gnarled tree trunk. There, you will be told, is where the Holy Family rested. Go up the Nile and you will find a string of places where the Holy Family is believed to have journeyed. Not only for Coptic Christians did the Holy Family flee into Egypt, they travelled throughout the land and made the whole land holy. And that scene of the Holy Family in Egypt is painted on many icons and celebrated in many ways.

Blake's 'Jerusalem' records the ancient legend of Joseph of Arimathea bringing the young child Jesus to England in the words: 'And was the holy Lamb of God on England's pleasant pastures seen?' How deep is this sense of wanting to find ways of saying that God is with us, that God is not an absent God but involved in the very particular places of our human lives. Yes, God is with us, for we stretch to receive Christ in the blessed sacrament, that he may dwell in our hearts and rule our lives. And so it is that Jerusalem may be built, not just in England's 'green and pleasant land' but throughout the world. For it is the Christ who dwells in us who enables us to find him in our neighbour and in those we meet day by day.

The Introit: *Omnis terra*

Let all the world worship thee, O God; let it sing of thee and praise thy name. O be joyful in God all ye lands: sing praises unto the honour of his name, make his praise to be glorious.

Mary:

Because Joseph had been warned of the vulnerability of infants to Herod's uncontrollable rage, which would rise up in a moment if a thought troubled him, we settled for a while in Egypt before carrying on to Nazareth following the death of Herod.

Already, after only a few weeks of my son's life, many had suffered through the murderous rage of one man.

For further consideration . . .

If I ignore my neighbour, I cannot see Christ in my neighbour.

Day 37

The Gospel of Matthew 2 : 15–18

And [Joseph] remained there until the death of Herod. This was to fulfil what the Lord had spoken by the prophet, 'Out of Egypt have I called my son.'

Then Herod, when he saw that he had been tricked by the wise men, was in a furious rage, and he sent and killed all the male children in Bethlehem and in all that region who were two years old and under, according to the time which he had ascertained from the wise men. Then was fulfilled what was spoken by the prophet Jeremiah: 'A voice was heard in Ramah, wailing and loud lamentation, Rachel weeping for her children; she refused to be consoled, because they were no more.'

(Herod thought nothing of the sacrifice of a few children to secure his throne. Indeed, at least two of his sons had been killed for the same reason.)

Reflection

Jesus warned his hearers again and again against making easy distinctions between themselves (the virtuous) and others (obvious sinners). For every murder committed there are thousands of instances of murderous hatred and hundreds of thousands of instances of life-sapping hatred. The innocent, in one way or another, have been massacred as a result. We know that this is the case, for at times we have been in the position of the innocent and have been on the receiving end; our only mistake in such circumstances is to imagine that we are always and completely the innocent. For we know how easy it is to establish ourselves in a powerful position of hurt innocence, the righteously aggrieved; and this is just as damaging to ourselves and others.

The helpless child, who was such a threat to the powerful Herod, whom Herod sought to eliminate by the massacre at Bethlehem, is, the Christian gospel proclaims, the Lord and Saviour of mankind. He saves both the innocent and the tyrant; both are called to share in the life and power of his kingdom, but both can only share in that kingdom if they acknowledge their need and their sin. The nature of that kingdom and its Lord is made clear by Paul when he urges the Philippians to live out 'the common life of Christ' which must be shown by love for each other, a care for unity, and an absence of rivalry and personal vanity. All this must arise out of 'your life in Christ Jesus' who 'did not think to snatch at equality with God, but made himself nothing, assuming the nature of a slave . . . and in obedience accepted death – even death on a cross.'

The Sequence: *Epiphaniam Domino*

Angel-warned, no word they bring back to Herod, ruthless king.
Maddened with exceeding ire forth he sends the mandate dire throughout Bethlehem's roads to seek and to slay the infants meek.

Mary:

As we prepare again to leave the Temple with, I think, a reluctant son, I wonder why children had to die to satisfy the anger of a king; to satisfy the instinct of those who would have God for themselves alone.

For further consideration . . .

In a furious rage, self is always at the forefront.

Day 38

The Gospel of Matthew 2 : 19–23

*But when Herod died, behold, an angel of the
Lord appeared in a dream to Joseph in Egypt, saying, 'Rise, take the child and his mother, and go to
the land of Israel, for those who sought the child's
life are dead.'*

*And he rose and took the child and his mother,
and went to the land of Israel. But when he heard
that Archelaus reigned over Judea in place of his
father Herod, he was afraid to go there, and being
warned in a dream he withdrew to the district of
Galilee.*

*And he went and dwelt in a city called
Nazareth, that what was spoken by the prophets
might be fulfilled, 'He shall be called a Nazarene.'*

(Herod died in 4 BC. The exile in Egypt is likely to
have lasted six months at the very least. Archelaus
had a not undeserved reputation for cruelty.)

Reflection

Egypt was a place of refuge for both the Children
of Israel and for the Holy Family. Yet for the
Children of Israel it became a place of slavery and
hardship from which they were led to freedom
through Moses, the deliverer, whom God raised

up. In his Gospel, Matthew draws a parallel between Moses and Jesus. Jesus is seen, in the Sermon on the Mount, as the new Moses, giving the new law, the new covenant, the new testament, on the mountain, the new Sinai. In the flight into Egypt, Matthew wishes us to see God in Christ retracing the pattern of deliverance of the Old Testament, of the Exodus journey. The Holy Family journey to Egypt as refugees, and from Egypt they return – and Matthew cites a verse of the Prophet Hosea, 'Out of Egypt have I called my son.' The 'son' in this case refers to Israel, so in Jesus the vocation of the people of God is fulfilled. Here is the true Son of God, called out of Egypt to be Saviour of both Israel and the whole world.

The Introit: *In excelso throno*

I saw seated on a high throne, a man whom a multitude of angels worshipped, chanting together, behold him, the name of whose kingdom is for everlasting.

Mary:

Leaving Egypt, we returned to Nazareth, even though we had still remotely entertained the thought of settling in Bethlehem. But prudence prevailed.

It strikes me now that as God called the children of Israel – his 'son' – from Egypt, whence they embarked upon an arduous journey to the promised land through the agency of Moses, so out of

Egypt, Jesus, the 'Son of the Most High' was called through the agency of Joseph to be brought up in Nazareth for a mission whose detail I cannot begin to imagine.

For further consideration . . .

Joseph's guardianship of Jesus was meticulous and dedicated.

Day 39

The Gospel of Matthew 3:1–3

In those days came John the Baptist, preaching in the wilderness of Judea, 'Repent, for the kingdom of heaven is at hand.' For this is he who was spoken of by the prophet Isaiah when he said, 'The voice of one crying in the wilderness: Prepare the way of the Lord, make his paths straight.'

(See note Day 24. John began his ministry in the arid and mountainous region east of the Jerusalem-Hebron road.)

Reflection

Only John the Baptist will recognize Jesus and point him out. But, before he is identified by John, he is just one of the crowd, hidden, unknown, indistinguishable from the press of those around him, seemingly an ordinary human being coming to a baptism of repentance and responding to God's call. That hiddenness and ordinariness is important.

The Russian writer, Turgenev, tells how he once had a dream about himself as a young lad, standing in an old country church amongst a peasant congregation. Suddenly, he was aware that someone had arrived and was standing behind him:

and, curiously, at once he felt that this man was Christ. He was over-awed and turned hesitantly to look ... 'A face like everyone's: a face like all men's faces. The eyes looked a little upwards, quietly and intently, the hands folded and still. And the clothes on him like everyone's. What sort of Christ is this? I thought, such an ordinary, ordinary man. It can't be.' The lad looked away but then felt impelled to turn once more ... 'Again, the same face, like all men's faces, the same everyday though unknown features. And suddenly my heart sank, and I came to myself. Only then did I realize that just such a face – a face like all men's faces – is indeed the face of Christ.'

Jesus comes to be baptized; coming as one of the crowds, coming as one of us.

The Antiphon: *Baptizat miles regem*

The soldier baptizeth the King, the servant his Master, the Baptist his redeemer: the water of the Jordan marvelled; the Dove bore witness.

Mary:

Today's events are so much a proper part of his preparation, I wince at my admonishment of him.

In the future, John will draw people's attention to Jesus and will make ready, make receptive, and cultivate the wilderness that is the mind of man.

For further consideration . . .

The face of Christ is often where we least expect to find it.

Day 40

The Gospel of Luke 2:41–52

Now his parents went to Jerusalem every year at the feast of the Passover. And when he was twelve years old, they went up according to custom; and when the feast was ended, as they were returning, the boy Jesus stayed behind in Jerusalem. His parents did not know it, but supposing him to be in the company they went a day's journey, and they sought him among their kinsfolk and acquaintances; and when they did not find him, they returned to Jerusalem, seeking him. After three days they found him in the temple, sitting among the teachers, listening to them and asking them questions; and all who heard him were amazed at his understanding and his answers. And when they saw him they were astonished; and his mother said to him, 'Son, why have you treated us so? Behold, your father and I have been looking for you anxiously.' And he said to them, 'How is it that you sought me? Did you not know that I must be in my Father's house?' And they did not understand the saying which he spoke to them. And he went down and came to Nazareth, and was obedient to them; and his mother kept all these things in her heart.

And Jesus increased in wisdom and in stature, and in favour with God and man.

(Pilgrimages were often made in groups or village parties.)

Reflection

Jesus came to Jerusalem in adolescence, on pilgrimage with his family and friends of the family. There he began to understand his own identity, an identity which seemed to demand going beyond that family. He discovered there the imperative of God. That was what lay at the heart of his life. In the Temple, the place of meeting with God, he wrestled and debated with the religious teachers, searching for what God might mean. And when Mary and Joseph find him in that place, the justification that he offers for his behaviour is that it is God who is his great concern, and God he dares to name as Father. In finding his way to independence, to his own identity, Jesus affirms his true dependence.

John tells us at the beginning of his Gospel that in seeing Jesus we see nothing less than God's glory, God's very character; and that is shown to us by the one who lives in utter closeness to God, in perfect obedience of Sonship.

Jesus grew up, advancing in wisdom 'and in favour with God and men'. And that is our calling too.

The Antiphon: *Remansit puer Iesus*

The child Jesus tarried behind in Jerusalem, and Joseph and his mother knew not of it, and they

sought him among their kinsfolk and acquaintances.

Mary:

I have scolded my son. In the act of so doing I had
to smile not only because I was, naturally enough,
happy and relieved but also at the ease with which
he conversed with the learned men. Was his reply
to me not to be expected? Was it surprising that
he was to be found in the Temple simultaneously
vexing and impressing, enraging and amazing the
theologians? This was his first visit and he was
most anxious to come. Why did we not know
precisely where he would be found?

My smiling prevails over my irritation as I
know that he must prepare for the vocation he has
been given. What a grasp of the prophets and the
law he already has – those very men who spoke so
eloquently about him.

For further consideration . . .

After three days Mary found Jesus in the Temple.
In twenty years or so she would find him again
after three days' absence in the tomb.

Day 41

(6 January – The Epiphany of Our Lord)

The Gospel of Matthew 2:7–11

Then Herod summoned the wise men secretly and ascertained from them what time the star appeared; and he sent them to Bethlehem, saying, 'Go and search diligently for the child, and when you have found him bring me word, that I too may come and worship him.' When they had heard the king they went their way; and lo, the star which they had seen in the East went before them, till it came to rest over the place where the child was. When they saw the star, they rejoiced exceedingly with great joy; and going into the house they saw the child with Mary his mother, and they fell down and worshipped him. Then, opening their treasures, they offered him gifts, gold, frankincense and myrrh.

The Gospel of Luke 3:21,22

Now when all the people were baptized, and when Jesus also had been baptized and was praying, the heaven was opened, and the Holy Spirit descended in bodily form, as a dove, and a voice came from heaven, 'Thou art my beloved Son; with thee I am well pleased.'

The Gospel of John 2:1–11

On the third day there was a marriage at Cana in Galilee, and the mother of Jesus was there; Jesus also was invited to the marriage, with his disciples. When the wine failed, the mother of Jesus said to him, 'They have no wine.' And Jesus said to her, 'O woman, what have you to do with me? My hour has not yet come.' His mother said to the servants, 'Do whatever he tells you.' Now six stone jars were standing there, for the Jewish rites of purification, each holding twenty or thirty gallons. Jesus said to them, 'Fill the jars with water.' And they filled them up to the brim. He said to them, 'Now draw some out, and take it to the steward of the feast.' So they took it. When the steward of the feast tasted the water now become wine, and did not know where it came from (though the servants who had drawn the water knew), the steward of the feast called the bridegroom and said to him, 'Every man serves the good wine first; and when men have drunk freely, then the poor wine; but you have kept the good wine until now.' This, the first of his signs, Jesus did in Cana in Galilee, and manifested his glory; and his disciples believed in him.

(The appearance of the Spirit over the waters of the Jordan is reminiscent of the creation story of Genesis and heralds the making known of the New Creation.

The apparent abruptness of Jesus' response to his mother at the wedding must not be misinterpreted. It was neither disrespectful nor a refusal, as evidenced by 'Do whatever he tells you.' If one imagines it said with a smile; that probably makes the best translation.)

Reflection

The Holy Family are there in Bethlehem waiting for the exotic men, about whom they know nothing, to arrive at the house, greet the baby with effusion, and leave unlikely and expensive presents. Mary and Joseph show the Christ-Child to the representatives of the Gentile world – that is, the rest of the world.

John the Baptist, according to the Gospel of John, identifies Jesus as 'The Lamb of God' to those round about. Jesus is unknown until he is pointed to and shown to those gathered around. The voice from heaven and the Spirit descending like a dove confirm his vocation and he is driven into the wilderness to wrestle with the conflict of possibilities for his ministry.

At the marriage in Cana, Jesus shows himself in this the first miracle, a metaphor for the out-pouring of his blood for the salvation of man, a revelation of the nature of his ministry.

What is it that we have been shown in Jesus? The impact of his Epiphany was the revelation of one who was God-possessed. The New Testament writers hold up to this strange and powerful figure a variety of mirrors, of different shapes and sizes and of different tints; some might be convex showing Jesus against the whole sweep of the universe, some concave, which focus the attention on what is seen. They all agree, however, that that God-possessed life is the fulfilment and the concentration of the Jewish experience of God the righteous and holy Creator, the Lord of the whole world, who yet cares for his people with a love so passionate that despite all their rebellion, he cannot give them up. Jesus is the point at which the inner transformation of human life, by the action of God who gave it being, has become a lived reality and, therefore, to have seen Jesus is to have been shown what God is like – the Word made flesh, God's communication of himself to us given expression in human terms from within a human life and worked out in the freedom of the obedience of a man created in the image of God. '. . . we have beheld his glory, glory as of the only Son from the Father.'

The Antiphon: *Fontes aquarum*

The springs of waters were hallowed when Christ appeared in majesty before the world: draw ye water from the wells of salvation; for now is every creature sanctified by Christ our God.

Mary:

Humanity is prevented from a return to Eden, a place intended for them, by flaming swords. Humanity's selfism was deserving of expulsion. Adam and Eve disobeyed God despite having had everything lavished upon them.

God made man and woman to be one flesh, to

live paradisially on easy terms with God and his creation. They were created in the image of God and with freedom of mind to choose their own selfish will, free to do good or ill. But in choosing themselves, they were no longer permitted the special garden: they had now to earn it (perhaps) or had to be saved for it by God himself.

God chose the family and seed of Abraham to show himself in the history of that family of nations. They were to find and follow the way of God and strive to find Eden again – a land promised by God, only to abuse the privilege yet again and to be expelled yet again.

My task is to bring up the 'Son of the Most High' to maturity. He was shown to the Jews at birth and to the nations of the world shortly afterwards: in maturity he will be pointed out by John, and then his words and deeds will speak for him and for themselves.

For further consideration . . .

If we see Christ in others, we see the Father.

Day 42

(2 February – Candlemas)

The Gospel of Luke 2 : 22–40

And when the time came for their purification according to the law of Moses, they brought him up to Jerusalem to present him to the Lord (as it is written in the law of the Lord, 'Every male that opens the womb shall be called holy to the Lord') and to offer a sacrifice according to what is said in the law of the Lord, 'a pair of turtledoves, or two young pigeons.' Now there was a man in Jerusalem, whose name was Simeon, and this man was righteous and devout, looking for the consolation of Israel, and the Holy Spirit was upon him. And it had been revealed to him by the Holy Spirit that he should not see death before he had seen the Lord's Christ. And inspired by the Spirit he came into the temple; and when the parents brought in the child Jesus, to do for him according to the custom of the law, he took him up in his arms and blessed God and said, 'Lord, now lettest thou thy servant depart in peace, according to thy word; for mine eyes have seen thy salvation which thou hast prepared in the presence of all peoples, a light for revelation to the Gentiles, and for glory to thy people Israel.'

And his father and his mother marvelled at

*what was said about him; and Simeon blessed
them and said to Mary his mother, 'Behold, this
child is set for the fall and rising of many in Israel,
and for a sign that is spoken against (and a sword
will pierce through your own soul also), that
thoughts out of many hearts may be revealed.'*

*And there was a prophetess, Anna, the daughter
of Phanuel, of the tribe of Asher; she was of a
great age, having lived with her husband seven
years from her virginity, and as a widow till she
was eighty-four. She did not depart from the
temple, worshipping with fasting and prayer night
and day. And coming up at that very hour she
gave thanks to God, and spoke to all who were
looking for the redemption of Jerusalem.*

*And when they had performed everything
according to the law of the Lord, they returned
into Galilee, to their own city, Nazareth. And the
child grew and became strong, filled with wisdom;
and the favour of God was upon him.*

(Simeon sees the promise to Abraham – that salvation is for all nations – here fulfilled. The light is
there for all to see.)

Reflection

Candlemas is a feast of vision; a feast of sight and
insight. The candles remind us of the light which
has broken into a world of darkness, where sin
distorts, and where the goodness of God's creation
is blotted out by human wickedness.

A child is taken to the Temple; taken by Mary

and Joseph to fulfil the rites of the law. An old
man is there, looking, searching, straining to see
the promise of redemption being fulfilled and the
dawning of the day of salvation. His rheumy eyes
search for a sign of hope in a despairing world. He
lives at a time of tension between God's promise
and a mocking world. And in his longing he is
drawn to the Temple, to that place where sacrifice
is offered, and where in costly giving men strive to
know their Maker. He comes into the Temple,
where the great veil or curtain, embroidered with
the signs of heaven, guards the mysterious empti-
ness of the Holy of Holies, the place where God is,
and yet is not, for God does not dwell in temples
made with hands. Simeon comes, looking, searching; and he sees a child, and he takes the child into
his arms and blesses God. His sight becomes
insight. He sees and knows in the child he carries
the promise of God fulfilled. Here is no less than
the one for whom not only Israel but all nations
long. He is 'a light to lighten the Gentiles, and the
glory of his people Israel.'

The Feast of Candlemas has many names. It is
the Feast of the Presentation of Christ; of the
Purification of the Blessed Virgin Mary; and in
the East it is known simply as The Meeting – the
meeting of Simeon with the infant Jesus, the meeting of God and Man as the Lord comes to his
Temple. Here in this meeting, Simeon sees and
knows the Christ of God; and that meeting is both
joy and sorrow: joy that the light shines in the
darkness and joy in the promise of salvation; and
sorrow at the cost of salvation. If we adore the

Lord as the Christ of God, and find in him a love that reaches the heart of human need, then we shall find as we come closer to him to share in his love and compassion that our adoration means a suffering with and alongside Christ. This will be so in many ways: in reaching out to the despairing and the angry and sharing with Christ in receiving and bearing their hatred; in patiently bearing misrepresentation, calumny and slander; in enduring beyond what is reasonable; in wrestling in prayer for those in need, those unloved, and those in pain of any kind. It is in praying deeply, and ever more deeply, that we can come to know and enter this sacrament of sacrificial love, this mystery in which Christ meets us in his Temple with the promise of salvation.

The Prose: *Ave! plena gratia*

Let thy servants now depart, let us see thee as thou art, naught of earth arrest our eyes.
But if here we stay below, in thee, Jesu, let us grow, so in thee we shall arise.

Mary:

For the second time, we prepare to move north, away from Jerusalem. This time, I think that Joseph will be sure to keep an eye upon the child to ensure that the journey is made without further surprise!

When I took Jesus for the first time to the Temple, he was held by Simeon with relief.

Simeon was happy then to die having seen, as he put it, 'the Lord's Christ'. As I have recalled a number of times, Simeon spoke of light shining upon all peoples of the world and, of course, upon the children of Israel. He saw further than his dim eyes, singularly lacking in light; he saw God's own light, God's promised light brightening the dark corners of space, of minds and lives.

For further consideration . . .

Candlemas is a feast of sight and insight.